CHINA

A NEW YORK TIMES BYLINE BOOK

SOUTHEAST ASIA by TILLMAN DURDIN
AFRICA by WALDEMAR A. NIELSEN
RUSSIA by HARRISON E. SALISBURY
CHINA by HARRY SCHWARTZ
LATIN AMERICA by TAD SZULC
THE MIDDLE EAST by JAY WALZ

NEW YORK TIMES BYLINE BOOKS

CHINA

by Harry Schwartz

A NEW YORK TIMES BYLINE BOOK

ATHENEUM

NEW YORK

1972

FOR RUTH

CONTENTS

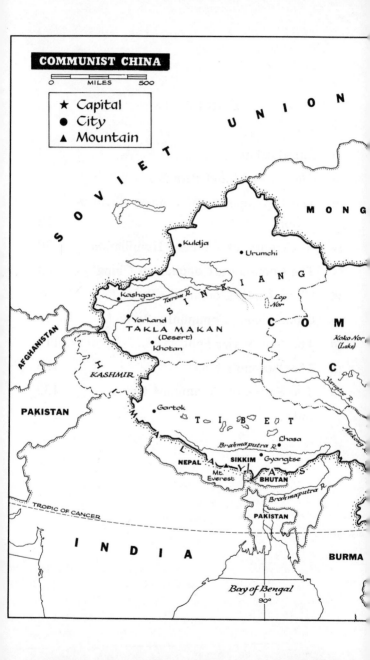

COMMUNIST CHINA

0 MILES 500

★ Capital
● City
▲ Mountain

SOVIET UNION

MONG

• Kuldja

• Urumchi

Kashgar

Tarim R.

SINKIANG

Lop Nor

COM

Yarkand

TAKLA MAKAN
(Desert)

Khotan

Koko Nor
(Lake)

AFGHANISTAN

KASHMIR

HIMA

PAKISTAN

Gartok

TIBET

Yangtse R.

Chasa

Brahmaputra R.

NEPAL

LAYA

SIKKIM

Gyangtse

Mt.
Everest

S

BHUTAN

Me

PAKISTAN

Brahmaputra R.

TROPIC OF CANCER

INDIA

BURMA

Bay of Bengal
90°

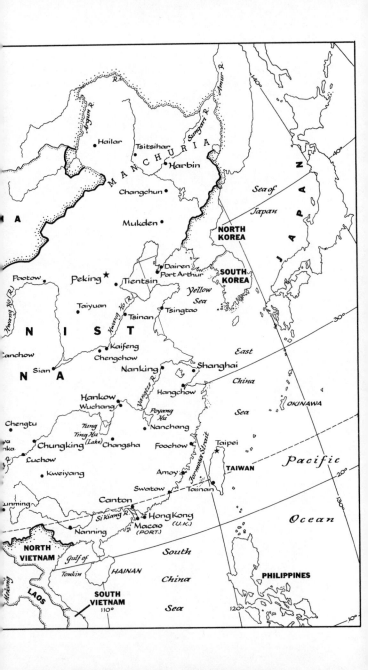

CHINA

A NEW YORK TIMES BYLINE BOOK

I

Introduction

ONE DAY in the summer of 1900 the front page of *The New York Times* reported startling news. "Chinese Shoot Straight," said the headline of an article about the Boxer Rebellion, a movement aimed at driving foreigners out of China. In Peking, China's capital, the Legation Quarter, where thousands of foreign families had sought refuge, was under siege. A breathless world waited to learn whether it could hold out (it ultimately did) until friendly troops arrived. In the siege, the article declared, the foreigners had learned to their cost that Chinese soldiers with guns in their hands were dangerous because they could shoot straight. The prominence *The Times* gave this information left no doubt that it was big news for Americans in 1900.

Now, in the nineteen-sixties, it seems almost incredible that as the 20th century began intelligent people should have been surprised that the Chinese could shoot straight. So different is our view of China today that the world was not surprised when Peking exploded its first atomic bombs in 1964 and 1965. Those events in fact, had been forecast earlier by the United States. Informed people know that Communist China's military power casts a dark shadow over all its neighbors from Southeast Asia and India to Siberia and Japan. In 1950 and 1951, during the first bitter winter of the Korean War, Americans learned the hard way what effective fighters the Chinese could be. Chinese troops poured into North Korea and drove the United Nations forces there, including tens of thousands of American soldiers, far southward before their advance was stopped. Further proof of Chinese military ability was provided in 1962 when China attacked India. In a few weeks Chinese troops, routing Indian forces, fought their way across the towering Himalayas almost to the plains of Assam. Then the Chinese, having demonstrated their power, halted and withdrew.

Communist China, the new giant in world affairs, has declared the United States to be its Number One enemy. Huge demonstrations denouncing the United States and its leaders are commonplace in Peking and other Chinese cities. Day after day

Chinese Communist propaganda dins into Chinese minds the thought that the United States is the most evil of lands. Hatred of the United States is taught to children virtually from the day they enter school. Americans can hardly be indifferent when the most populous country of the world systematically cultivates among its people enmity toward the United States.

In March, 1965, when it became known that the United States had made occasional and isolated use of non-deadly gas against Communist forces in South Vietnam, an editorial in Peking's chief newspaper stated:

In its war of aggression against South Vietnam, the Johnson Administration has directly employed the U.S. Air Force and ground troops, repeatedly bombed North Vietnam and done what the Eisenhower and Kennedy Administrations did not dare to do. Now it has gone to the extent of using poisonous gas and done what even Hitler did not dare to do. Facts prove that Lyndon Johnson, chieftain of the U.S. imperialist gangsters, is the most brutal war criminal of our time. . . . The United States not only uses gas against combat personnel, but also adopts this means to kill the unarmed and innocent civilians, including the old, the feeble, women and children. The

United States has committed such a monstrous crime, but still talks about "humanity." What shame! . . . Lyndon Johnson will not escape the punishment he deserves for this monstrous war crime.

Yet an enormous amount of ignorance about China exists in our nation. A 1964 survey, for example, found that many Americans lack the most elementary information about China. Tens of millions apparently do not even know that Mainland China is now under Communist rule, though that has been true since 1949.

There are reasons for such lack of knowledge. One is that the Chinese Communist Government has for years excluded virtually all Americans from China. Washington and Peking do not accord each other diplomatic recognition, and United States newspaper correspondents are not allowed to enter Mainland China. *The New York Times,* for example, has long sought without success to get reporters in.

However, Americans who want to can still learn a great deal about Communist China. The Chinese publish in English and send abroad many books and magazines. These publications present Peking's official version of events and contain much propaganda, but they can be checked against the reports of non-Communists who have been allowed to visit Communist China. Peking has permitted Canadians, Englishmen, Frenchmen, Germans, Japanese and others to enter, and many of these visitors have written about their experiences. *The New York Times* often publishes dispatches from Communist China by Reuters, a British news service, and articles by Canadian and other Western correspondents who have gained admission to the country. Moreover, many Chinese have escaped and taken refuge in Hong Kong, Japan and elsewhere. Their accounts of life under Communist rule are frequently illuminating. From these and other reports we can and do learn a great deal about what goes on in Peking's domains.

The Chinese Communist hostility to the United States is so important that it is worth at the very outset considering the reasons for it. One is that the United States Seventh Fleet, stationed off the coast of China, helps protect the Nationalist Chinese regime of Chiang Kai-shek, which rules the Island of Taiwan, often called Formosa. Peking charges that the United States has actually seized Taiwan from China and says the "return of Taiwan" is an essential requirement for the improvement of relations. Washington rejects the charge as nonsense. Beyond the Taiwan issue, the Chinese Communists now view the United States as the chief Western colonial power in Asia, claiming that Washington seeks to reimpose the control over

Asian peoples once held by the British, French and Dutch. The presence of American troops in South Vietnam, South Korea and Japan is cited by Chinese Communist propaganda as "proof" of American imperialism. Peking prefers to ignore the fact that American troops are in these countries by agreement with their governments, which look to the United States for help in preserving their independence against Chinese or other aggression.

Many older Americans find the bitter hostility between the United States and the rulers of Communist China hard to accept. They remember the years before 1949, when the United States thought of itself as a special friend of China. During World War II the United States shipped many millions of dollars' worth of arms and supplies to help China in the war against Japan. Before that war, Americans helped build schools, colleges and hospitals in China, and we sent doctors, teachers and missionaries there. During the same period thousands of young Chinese attended schools and colleges in the United States. Recalling this, many Americans were startled by China's open hostility to the United States during the past 15 years.

We know now that such attitudes were based on illusions which ignored the realities of China. Valuable as American doctors and teachers were, they barely scratched the surface of China's enormous needs, and most Chinese probably were never even aware of their work. Some observers suggest that the missionaries made more enemies than friends, because many Chinese resented the idea of foreigners trying to convert them. This dislike was strengthened by the special privileges enjoyed by the missionaries and their converts. It may help if we think of what the American reaction would have been if Chinese missionaries had come here to convert Americans to Confucianism, and if these missionaries and their converts enjoyed special privileges denied the mass of Americans. The average Chinese, we may suspect, had little if any basis for differentiating Americans from other white men in China, and he tended to resent these foreigners with their superior wealth, power and high standard of living.

During and immediately after World War II, the United States did occupy a special place in China because of our military and economic aid. In the mid-nineteen-forties the American position was so influential that it was possible for General George Marshall to seek a compromise between the regime of Chiang Kai-shek and its Communist opponents. But the Marshall mission failed, and when the Communists won the civil war they looked at the United States with the bitterness born of the conviction that we had been the main support—military, economic and moral—of Chiang Kai-shek. Against this background Mao Tse-tung announced his "lean to one side" policy, the position of favoring the Soviet Union against the United States in world politics.

The outbreak of the Korean War in 1950 helped solidify Communist Chinese hostility. President Truman ordered the Seventh Fleet to protect Taiwan against Communist invasion from the mainland. The Communists in Peking saved North Korea from defeat by sending in tens of thousands of Chinese soldiers—posing as "volunteers"—who inflicted a major defeat on American and other United Nations troops in the dark winter of 1950–1951. Hostility between the two countries has been great ever since, yet Washington and Peking still maintain some formal channel of diplomatic communication, even though they do not recognize each other. American and Chinese diplomats have been meeting in Warsaw, Poland, several times a year to discuss matters of common interest. The meetings usually last only a few hours, and the proceedings are chilly. Yet the fact that these meetings take place keeps open the opportunity for improved relations.

Not only the United States but every major government pays a good deal of attention to the Peking regime and its policies. Increasingly, Communist China is establishing diplomatic, trade and other ties with various countries, and its influence has mounted in Africa and parts of Latin America as well as in Asia—witness the accusations of Peking's involvement in the bloody rebellion that swept the northern Congo in late 1964. Moreover, Communist China's bitter rift with the Soviet Union in recent years has wrecked the former unity of the world Communist movement and set Communist to fighting Communist in many countries.

Apart from all this, there are three fundamental reasons why anyone ought to be interested in China:

First, it is the world's most populous nation. Its 700 million people make up almost one-quarter of humanity. Their number is three and a half times that of the population of the United States. Before the end of this century, if current trends continue, China will have well over a billion people. Will this crowded country be content to stay within its own borders and make do with its own resources, or will it seek more living space by seizing territory from its neighbors?

Second, a great drama of modern times is under way in China. For a long time the Chinese have been, as they are now, among the poorest people on earth. In this century the typical Chinese has had to exist on an annual income of less than $100. This is a level of poverty that Americans—who have on the average more than $2,500 a year each on which to live—find difficult even to imagine. The Communist leaders of China are sworn to lift their nation from past weakness, backwardness and desti-

tution into a new era of strength, industrial power
and relative plenty. If Communist rule in China
can accomplish this in a reasonably short period—
say, a few decades—the effect on the hundreds of
millions of people in other poor and underdeveloped lands in Asia, Africa and Latin America will
be profound. But if the effort fails, the appeal of
Communism on these continents will diminish
sharply.

Finally, China—whether under Communist or
non-Communist rule—is one of the most fascinat-
ing countries in the world. Of all the great nations
China has the longest continuous history and culture. The United States is less than 200 years old, but
the Chinese people can trace their national history
back more than 4,000 years. Chinese civilization—
notably its philosophy, literature, art and, in some
periods, science—has for millenniums represented
one of the peaks of human accomplishment. It was
the Chinese who invented gunpowder, paper, the
compass, the basic technology of printing. A thousand years and more ago, when Europe lay in the
grip of the Dark Ages, the Chinese were making
systematic observations of the heavens, obtaining
data that modern astronomers still use. Some ac-
quaintance with China's history and culture is essential for a truly educated person.

This volume seeks to provide a brief introduc-
tion to China, its role in the modern world and its

importance for the future. The emphasis will be upon the present and the recent past, but neither can be understood without looking first at the foundation stones of the contemporary Chinese Communist state: the land, the people, the ancient traditions and the new ideology. To these we now turn.

II

China's Land and People

MANY IN THE WEST were surprised in the late nineteen-forties when the Chinese Communist party under Mao Tse-tung conquered Mainland China. But, looking backward, we can see now that the surprise was excessive. The great poverty of the Chinese people provided fertile ground for the ideas planted by Communist agitators. In addition, there was much in China's traditions, as we shall discover later, that facilitated the triumph of Mao's brand of Marxism. As for the poverty, it can largely be explained by the relationship between China's land and people.

An ordinary map of China is deceptive, for it shows a vast country of almost four million square miles, a country bigger than the United States. Its

north-south extension is equivalent to the distance
between Puerto Rico and Labrador. Its maximum
east-west length is greater than the distance between New York and Los Angeles. Even with 700
million people, the map suggests, China should
still have plenty of room. If we divide the area by
the number of people, we find about 175 Chinese
to the square mile. New York State has almost
twice as many inhabitants per square mile, and
Rhode Island is far more crowded than China theoretically is.

Such comparisons, however, are highly mislead-
ing, for they leave out a key factor: Most of China's territory consists of mountains and deserts that
are inhospitable to human habitation and that—so
far, at least—have contributed little to the country's
wealth. Three out of four Chinese are concentrated
in only 15 per cent of the country, mainly in the
east and south, while much of the rest of China is
virtually empty. The heartland consists of the great
valleys through which the Yellow River and the
Yangtze flow. In these densely packed regions and
some similar ones near Canton and elsewhere along
the coasts, the census takers commonly find 1,000
to 2,000 people per square mile and in the most
crowded of these areas 2,500 to 3,000 people per
square mile. But elsewhere in China, in such western and northern segments as Tibet, Sinkiang and
Inner Mongolia, population is sparse and vast tracts

have fewer than 10 people per square mile.

Over large areas of the United States an average-size family farm will vary between, say, 200 and 500 acres, or roughly between one-third and five-sixths of a square mile. Such an American farm will support a family of four, five or six people and perhaps a hired worker or two as well. But in the jampacked agricultural heartland of China, the typical peasant family must live off the equivalent of one, two or three acres. On acreage that a Kansas wheat farmer or a Nebraska corn grower would consider moderate or even small, there will live in China 1,000 or more people, all of them eking out a scanty living by intensive cultivation of every available square inch of ground. That the Chinese have been able to survive and multiply in these heartland regions for thousands of years is testimony to how hard they have worked, to the expert and traditionally loving care they have given their land and to the courage with which they have met repeated misfortune. For in China natural disasters have been frequent, among them devastating floods, typhoons and droughts. The perennial struggle to raise enough food for himself and his family has been the central concern of the Chinese peasant and still is today.

From this point of view there are really two Chinas. One is the aforementioned heartland, embracing most of the people, most of the food production and almost all of the important cities. This is the area enclosed in the rough triangle that would be formed by a line drawn southwest from Harbin in the northeast through Peking to Chungking and then southeast to the shoreline and on to Hainan Island. This triangle and the coasts east and south of it form the China we usually think of. But west and north is the second China, the arid and mountainous areas that make up most of the country. Here there are relatively few people and comparatively little conventional farming. The familiar figure is the herdsman tending his cattle or sheep.

The line separating the heartland and the vast western and northern reaches is more than a division between regions of intensive farming and areas of livestock raising, or between river valleys and rolling plains on the one hand and mountains and deserts on the other. It is also a division between the homelands of the Chinese and non-Chinese segments of the population. Those we call Chinese are the Han people. They make up more than 90 per cent of the population; it is their language and culture we mean when we speak of the Chinese language and the Chinese culture. But besides the Han Chinese there are about 35 million to 40 million Chinese citizens who belong to non-Chinese (that is, non-Han) minorities, peoples with their own languages, cultures and histories who have not been assimilated by the Han as have so many others in past centuries. Even 50 years ago China's western and northern borderlands were dominated by these minority peoples, much as the Indians dominated the western United States for decades after the American Revolution. But just as the white man's steady progress westward in our country finally crowded out the Indians, many of whom now live on reservations, so the westward migration of the Han Chinese is increasingly taking over the lands of China's minorities.

A good way to take a look at these minorities is to move counterclockwise around China's periphery, starting with Manchuria in northeastern China. This is the ancestral home of the Manchus, who gave China its last dynasty but of whom the 1953 census found only about 2.4 million. In Manchuria and Inner Mongolia to the west are most of China's 1.5 million Mongols, descendants of the proud people who once conquered most of Europe and Asia under Genghis Khan and his successors. China's Mongols are culturally and historically related to the Mongols of Outer Mongolia, now officially the Mongolian People's Republic, but a closely guarded border separates the two branches of the Mongol people. In Sinkiang, which some foreigners have called China's Wild West, the key minorities include more than 3.5 million Uigurs, half a million Kazakhs and smaller numbers of Kirgiz and Tadzhik people. The presence of these Moslem minorities in Sinkiang has produced a particularly knotty political problem because substantial numbers of these same peoples live just over the border in Soviet Central Asia. In recent years Peking has accused Moscow of having encouraged rebellion among these non-Chinese minorities and of having urged them to flee from China to the Soviet Union after their rebellion failed. South of Sinkiang is Tibet, the fabled Buddhist land bordering on India and Nepal. Anti-Chinese guerrillas are still occasionally reported fighting in Tibet. Farther east, in the areas bordering on Burma and Vietnam, is the largest single non-Chinese minority —more than 6.5 million Chuang. Here too are the Yi people, who numbered more than 3.25 million in 1953. Numerically these and smaller minorities do not seem very significant, but they represent sources of actual or potential tension. They have rebelled against Chinese rule more than once, and today's masters in Peking know they may cause trouble again.

Up to this point it may seem that China consists only of farmers and herdsmen and that its people do nothing but raise crops or livestock. This is not true, of course, for China has great cities and growing industries. We have no recent data, but perhaps 100 million people—roughly 15 per cent of China's population—live in cities and towns today. China's largest metropolis is the great port and manufacturing center of Shanghai, which has more than six million people. Peking, with half that number, legitimately claims to have more beauty and art within its boundaries than any other city in the world. The capital of China for most of the last 700 years, it steadily accumulated art treasures as generation after generation built palaces and temples, gardens and parks. Each emperor sought to outdo his predecessors, and so for centuries China's best architects, sculptors and artists found employment adding new grace and beauty to the city. Near Peking is Tientsin, a great manufacturing center and second as a port only to Shanghai. In Manchuria, Harbin and Mukden reflect the rapid expansion of population this past half century. In the south, Canton is the leading port, the center from which most of the millions of overseas Chinese now influential in so many countries originally emigrated. There are other major cities, notably Nanking, Wuhan and Chungking, all on the Yangtze River. Many smaller cities have grown rapidly since Chinese Communist industrialization began in the early nineteen-fifties. But the typical Chinese is still a peasant, and it will be many decades before China's city dwellers outnumber its rural folk.

A word should be said here too about China's borders, on three of which there has been friction. The longest frontier, which runs several thousand miles and is interrupted by Outer Mongolia, separates the Soviet Union and Communist China. The Russians have charged in recent years that thousands of Chinese infiltrators have violated the border and tried to seize Soviet territory, especially islands in the Amur River. Chinese charges revolve around alleged Soviet ambitions to seize territory in Sinkiang in northwestern China. This is one of the tensest frontiers in the world, and there is much evidence to suggest that shooting incidents between Chinese and Soviet border guards are by no means rare. Tension exists along the border between Communist China and Mongolia too, for the Mongolian Government has supported the Soviet Union in the political and ideological struggle between Moscow and Peking. On China's border with India, Chinese claims on territory traditionally considered part of India erupted in major fighting in 1962. That fighting is over, but as a result of it the Chinese now occupy an area the Indians believe belongs to them. This border may again explode into violent conflict.

III

The Development of Chinese Civilization

AN ITALIAN PRIEST, Father Matthew Ricci, the Jesuit missionary who reopened Europe's intellectual contact with China more than 350 years ago, once wrote:

The Chinese look upon all foreigners as illiterate and barbarous, and refer to them in just these terms. They even disdain to learn anything from the books of outsiders because they believe that all true science and knowledge belongs to them alone. If perchance they have occasion to make mention of [foreigners] in their own writings, they treat them as though there was no room for doubt that they differ but little from the beasts of the field and the forest. Even the written characters by which they express the word "foreigner" are those that are applied to beasts.

Father Ricci had come to China to convert the heathen but soon discovered that the nation he was visiting regarded itself as the pinnacle of civilization, as the society from which all others should learn if they wished to elevate themselves from their base "barbarian" status. It differed little in essentials from the China Marco Polo had visited three centuries earlier, and this was not surprising, for much in Chinese civilization was basically fixed before the birth of Christ and has survived little changed. That civilization provides the foundation for Communist rule in the modern era, but even the transformations wrought by Communism have not eradicated ways of thought, national attitudes and other important attributes of earlier periods.

The basic pattern of Chinese society over the centuries has been that of a dictatorship ruled by a hereditary emperor with the help of officials chosen, theoretically at least, from the wisest men in the land. Emperors and dynasties could be and were overthrown, to be replaced by other emperors and other dynasties, but continuity was preserved because from generation to generation—until the beginning of this century—the officials who controlled the country shared the same values as their predecessors and were chosen in the same way. Chinese officials were scholars. They had to be, because they were selected by means of examinations which tested primarily their knowledge and understanding of the ancient philosophical classics. The higher the post an official aspired to, the more difficult the examination he had to pass and, consequently, the longer and more intensively he had to study the classics.

All China, Father Ricci wrote in obvious amazement, "is administered by the Order of the Learned, commonly known as the Philosophers. The responsibility for orderly management of the entire realm is wholly committed to their charge and care."

The man whose work was the foundation of this system of rule by scholars was Confucius, a thinker whose ideas have probably affected more human beings over the centuries than have those of any other builder of a philosophical structure. Confucius was born more than 2,500 years ago, in 551 B.C., and died in 478 B.C. Thus, he lived, worked, wrote and died before the golden age of Greek philosophy. Socrates, Plato and Aristotle lived after Confucius, but apparently never heard of him and his teachings.

Confucius was primarily interested in how men might live together so there should be peace and harmony. His emphasis was on good manners and ethical conduct. His basic assumption was that the nation or state was essentially an expanded family; the emperor could be regarded as the father, and his subjects as his children. He stressed the importance of a virtuous ruler who set a good example, saying to one monarch: "If your desire is for good, the people will be good. The moral character of the ruler is the wind; the moral character of those beneath him is the grass. When the grass has the wind upon it, it assuredly bends."

Confucius' philosophy, which bade the ruler deal "with the mass of the people as children," was essentially a code for the guidance of an absolute but hopefully benevolent dictatorship. It encouraged men to believe that if they followed the code, if their manners were correct and they exhibited virtue, they might attain China's supposedly lost Utopia, or Great Commonwealth, which was described in these terms:

When the Great Way was followed, everything under heaven was governed for the benefit of all the people. The ruler chose officials of virtue and ability, who dealt with their fellow men in righteous sincerity and harmony. Men, therefore, did not love only their own parents nor nurture only their own children. The aged were cherished until their deaths; those in their prime had employment suitable to their talents; and children grew up in suitable conditions. The people showed love and kindness to orphans, widows, to the [aged] childless and to those stricken by disabling diseases. All human beings received proper care. Men had their work, and women had their homes.

There was an abundance of wealth. . . . But the individual did not accumulate goods solely for his personal gratification. Realizing that it was wrong not to do so, everyone worked as hard as he could. But he did not exert his energies only for his own benefit. There was therefore no reason for men to scheme or plot, and men did not contend against each other. . . . There were neither thieves nor rebels pillaging the land, for each man had his proper place. When men threw open their front gates and never felt the need to close them again, that was the time of what we call the Great Commonwealth.

By directing men's attention toward the past and enjoining them to try to recover a lost utopia, Confucianism proved a profoundly conservative philosophy. Over the centuries the scholars who had to memorize the basic texts and study the commentaries upon them tended to assume that all that was important was already known. They were consequently suspicious of change and innovation. This attitude was the basis of the prideful arrogance which prevailed in the China Father Ricci described. It explained why the Chinese were so slow to acknowledge that the West had some ideas and technology which surpassed their own and would have to be learned if China were to survive.

Confucianism was not only a system of government, but also an attitude toward the universe and a quasi-religious system. It was profoundly agnostic, seeing little place or need for the idea of God and centering its attention upon man. Confucius tolerated the sacrifices the common man made to the spirits he thought ruled the world, but the sec-.ondary role Confucius attributed to such matters was apparent in his answer to a disciple who asked him about his duties to the spirits: "When still unable to do your duty to men, how can you do your duty to the spirits?" And his philosophy discouraged speculation about death or life after death. The sage was quoted as having told a student who asked about the nature of death: "Not yet understanding life, how can you understand death?" The emphasis was clearly on this world, on living the good life, not on death and what might come after it.

For Confucius and the hundreds of millions influenced by his teachings down through time, the central institution in human existence was the family and one's place in it during life and in death. One dutifully fulfilled one's obligations in the family scheme of things, venerated one's ancestors and helped bring forth children who would in turn be dutiful, obey their father and venerate their ancestors. This philosophy is directly opposed to the Western emphasis upon the individual, his worth and his uniqueness. For Confucius and for Chinese civilization the individual is only one link in an endless chain stretching back into the misty past and forward into the unknown future. The subordination of self to family obligations and to the need for continuing the chain of life indefinitely is fundamental to Confucianism.

The stress placed here upon Confucius and his teachings does not mean that Chinese civilization remained static for thousands of years or that unchanged Confucianism continued to be the only creed. On the contrary, Confucianism was challenged at times by rival doctrines—notably by Taoism, with its emphasis upon magic, and by Buddhism, which stressed contemplation and the attainment of nirvana, or freedom from passions and delusion. Buddhism exerted enormous influence at different periods. Moreover, the passage of the centuries saw many ideas penetrate China from the outside, especially under the Mongol emperors and during the Manchu Dynasty. But Chinese civilization was so comprehensive that until its contact with the disintegrating influence of the West it could absorb new and strange philosophies, modify them and finally incorporate them into an expanded but still basically Confucian system.

Much more might be said about the nature of Chinese civilization, but enough has been presented to show that it contained elements that made Communism more congenial and less strange than might be thought. Long before Mao Tse-tung the Chinese were habituated to believe that there was only one correct doctrine and that rule belonged to the learned who best understood and could best apply it. Long before Mao the Chinese had a vision of a utopia and believed it was man's duty to try to attain it. And long before Mao, too, the Chinese accepted the idea of absolute obedience to absolute rulers. When Mao taught his Communist disciples that their task was "to make Marxism Chinese," he must have had these helpful precedents in mind. His goal, which he achieved, was to become the latest of the traditional Chinese emperors, ruling with the aid of a Marxism modified to make it fuse with Confucianism. From our present perspective we can see that the Chinese people adopted Mao's strange fusion of doctrines after realizing that traditional Confucianism was inadequate for the 20th century and failing to find a more satisfactory alternative.

IV

A Century of Chinese Humiliation

THE COMMUNIST CONQUEST of China climaxed a century of Chinese humiliation by the West. That humiliation underlies the bitterness and hatred of Western nations shown so often by Peking in the nineteen-sixties. Many times before Mao Tse-tung assumed power, Chinese leaders had expressed their deep resentment at the way in which their country was being despoiled and divided by the great powers. Thus, the famed middle-class reformer Sun Yat-sen voiced his dismay in 1924 by declaring that China's people "are just a heap of loose sand. . . . Today we are the poorest and weakest nation in the world, and occupy the lowest position in international affairs. Other men are the carving knife and serving dish; we are the fish and the meat. Our position at this time is most perilous . . . there is danger of China's being lost and our people being destroyed."

These words contrasted strongly with what had been traditional Chinese pride and arrogance. They showed the effect on patriotic Chinese of almost 100 years of repeated military defeat and victimization by foreign powers. The search for ways to end foreign domination and restore China to a position of dignity in the world preoccupied many of the country's best minds after the middle of the 19th century. Marxism claims to be an international creed, but the Chinese Communists finally triumphed in part because of nationalism, because they convinced many of their people that they might be able to restore to China its ancient prestige and honor. The Communist take-over in 1949 was deeply rooted in the nationalism that grew out of China's ordeals after 1840.

Britain, Russia and France were the leaders in battering down the walls of Chinese isolation in the mid-19th century. They were later joined by Japan, Germany and the United States. All these nations wanted opportunities for profitable trade and investment in China, and most sought territorial gains as well, even hoping to divide China among themselves and end its existence as an independent state. Such attitudes were typical during the Age of Imperialism in the late 19th and early

20th centuries, when it was deemed normal for the strong to rule the weak. The great powers competed fiercely with one another in building up vast colonial empires in Asia and Africa. To some extent the Western assault upon China's former isolation had a religious basis as well: the desire to spread Christianity among the Chinese. But economic and territorial greed was the more usual motive.

In the 17th and 18th centuries very few Westerners had been permitted to visit China and fewer still had been allowed to settle there. It required much wrangling and conflict for Czarist Russia to win the right to send periodic trading caravans overland to Peking. The nations of the West—Britain and Portugal foremost among them—who reached China by sea were permitted only precarious and tiny footholds in specially designated areas on the coast. The Chinese emperors saw no reason to have extensive relations with the "barbarians" and knew virtually nothing about the distant lands from which the traders came to China. The emperors and the mandarins who served them thought of Britain, for example, as comparable to Siam. They were irritated at the contrast between the Siamese, who meekly brought tribute and prostrated themselves before the emperor, and the British, who sought relations based on equality and resisted suggestions that they kowtow to the emperor. The Chinese feeling of superiority was strengthened by the great European demand for tea and by the large quantities of silver bullion the Europeans brought to China to pay for the tea.

A clash was probably inevitable between the European nations, insistent on being treated as equals by the Chinese and determined that their merchants be given maximum opportunity for trade, and the Chinese, who sought to maintain their isolation in blissful ignorance of how strong the "barbarians" were. The great tragedy—one that has cast a terrible shadow over China's relations with the West ever since—is that the clash occurred over an issue on which the West's position was morally indefensible by today's standards: the British demand that the Chinese Government permit Western merchants to sell opium freely to Chinese. Since the eighteen-twenties these merchants had been eagerly pressing the opium trade, seeing in it a welcome source of profits and an alternative to silver in paying for Chinese tea. As opium addiction spread in China, the emperor and his advisers became ever more alarmed at the damage to Chinese health. A decision was taken to end the trade in opium. That decision brought on the conflict between Britain and China which is called the Opium War of 1839–1842.

Britain's naval power triumphed easily. The British saved the opium trade and ended China's isolation. With Chinese weakness revealed, Peking was forced by Western pressure to open more ports to trade, to permit Westerners to live within the country and to tolerate the activities of Christian missionaries. The principle of extraterritoriality was instituted. Under it foreigners committing crimes on Chinese territory were not subject to the jurisdiction of Chinese courts; they could be tried only in courts of their own country.

As the 19th century progressed, the Western surge into China became a flood. In 1860 British and French troops captured Peking, looted many of its treasures and destroyed the lovely Summer Palace. Increasingly, Britain, France, Germany, Japan and Russia competed in seizing or dominating Chinese territory. Japan took Korea. The French got Indochina, the area that now consists of North and South Vietnam, Laos and Cambodia. Russia seized vast regions in what is now Soviet Central Asia and the Soviet Far East, penetrated deeper into Manchuria and turned hungry eyes on Mongolia. The Germans established themselves as masters of the Shantung Peninsula. The British got Hong Kong, and British influence was the dominant force over a large part of China proper. As the 19th century ended, it seemed inevitable to many that China would be divided among the imperialist powers. As for the United States, it was a latecomer on the scene and called for an "open door" policy, demanding permission for American businessmen to trade and invest in every part of China.

As China's military impotence became ever clearer with the passage of time and permitted increasing foreign encroachment, the Chinese people grew angry at the indignities being inflicted upon them. Chinese fury was particularly directed at the Christian missionaries, who provided many valuable educational and medical services but also sought and won converts. Many of the Chinese who became Christians were considered traitors by other Chinese. In part this scorn arose from the special protection accorded the converts to safeguard them against persecution. Moreover, many Chinese believed the converts were nothing but "rice Christians" who had changed their religion only to get food and other material advantages. From time to time riots against the Chinese Christians testified to the jealousy and resentment the conversions had evoked. The climate was ideal for the growth of the poisonous flowers of Chinese xenophobia, a hatred of the foreigners whose power had so rudely disturbed the traditional Chinese way of life and humbled both the people and their rulers.

For decades the best minds of China sought ways to rebuild the nation's strength, drive out the foreign invaders and regain the might and majesty their country had enjoyed in the past. As early as 1861 the Chinese statesman Feng Kuei-fen pointed the way, declaring: "We have only one thing to learn from the barbarians, and that is strong ships and effective guns. . . . Funds should be allotted to establish a shipyard and arsenal in each trading port. A few barbarians should be employed, and Chinese who are good in using their minds should be selected to receive instruction so that in turn they may teach many craftsmen. . . . The intelligence and ingenuity of the Chinese are certainly superior to those of the various barbarians; it is only that hitherto we have not made use of them."

Feng and others who advocated change in 19th-century China ran into opposition from the traditional Confucianists. These conservatives feared that China would change radically if it embraced the technology and ideas of the West. How, they asked, could the profoundly conservative Chinese tradition, enforced by a ruling class selected for its knowledge of classics written hundreds and thousands of years earlier, be preserved if the validity of Western learning were conceded? But while the debate went on, the foreigners made deeper inroads on Chinese territory and independence. In June, 1898, the reformers won a temporary victory when they persuaded the young Manchu emperor to decree a great number of changes. The reforms ranged from the establishment of a free press to the requirement that would-be Government officials know Western subjects as well as the Confucian classics and take examinations in both. But the conservatives, under the leadership of the colorful Dowager Empress who dominated the last years of the Manchu Dynasty, struck back quickly to save the old ways. They organized a military coup, imprisoned the emperor and ended the short-lived attempt at reform from within. However, the conservatives' cause—that of stemming the onrushing tide of change—was really hopeless, and their triumph was brief indeed.

Without the military power they needed to give them bargaining strength in negotiations with foreigners, Chinese diplomats at the end of the 19th century had only one weapon: to get the greedy foreigners to fight one another and thus neutralize the might of each. This tactic scored some successes, but was ineffective when the foreigners agreed on the division of Chinese spoils among themselves. Desperately the Dowager Empress looked for a better way to humble the hated foreigners and reduce their power or drive them out.

Her eyes eventually lighted upon the "Society of Righteous, Harmonious Fists," better known as the Boxers, an organization that had gathered strength among the ignorant and superstitious peasantry during the late eighteen-nineties. The Boxer leaders claimed to have access to magical incantations and spells that made their followers invulnerable to bullets or other weapons. Under the slogan "Support the Manchus, Drive Out the Foreigners," the

Boxer leaders gathered thousands of recruits to fight the hated outsiders and kill the equally hated Chinese Christians. Initially the Boxers had been rebels, but as the movement gained strength the Dowager Empress grasped at the hope that it might be the answer to her prayers. She decided to support the Boxers and declare war against the nations preying on China.

The result was the Boxer Rebellion of 1900, and, as might have been expected, it was a disaster for China. Despite all their magic spells, the Boxers proved just as vulnerable to bullets as anyone else. They killed many Chinese Christians and a much smaller number of foreigners and besieged the Legation Quarter of Peking during the summer of 1900. But joint action by British, French, Japanese, Russian and other foreign troops soon defeated both the Boxers and the regular Chinese forces. The collapse of the Chinese effort forced the Dowager Empress to flee Peking until a settlement could be arranged. More important, it made China's weakness still more glaringly evident and strengthened the foreign grip on the country's territory, economy and resources. Even the Dowager Empress realized at last that China could not survive without change. Soon she began ordering reforms very much in the spirit of those that had been urged in 1898. The examination system was abolished as a means of choosing officials. The Government decided to start sending bright young men abroad to learn Western ways. A major effort to build a modern army was begun, and picked officers were sent to Japan for training. But this conversion had come too late to save the Manchu Dynasty. A revolution broke out in 1911; and in February, 1912, the reigning boy emperor, Pu-yi, abdicated. Thus ended 268 years of Manchu rule.

The fall of the Manchus and the proclamation of a Chinese Republic symbolized a triumph for radical reformers. They believed that China had to make a sharp break with the past and model itself on the West to be strong enough to regain an honorable place among the world's nations. But the great hopes originally entertained were grievously disappointed in the period between 1912 and the Communist conquest of the mainland in 1949. During those 37 years there was either civil war or war against a foreign invader or both. The Chinese people paid heavily for the disorder of that era.

Immediately after the Manchu abdication the most powerful man in China was Yuan Shih-kai, a former leading official and army commander under the Manchus. But he spent his energies seeking to be crowned emperor and thus to found a new dynasty, an effort which failed. Power soon became fragmented among a host of provincial warlords who quickly fell to fighting one another. Amid this confusion Japan took advantage of World War I to try to make all of China a Japanese colony. Even earlier the Russians had taken advantage of the increased Chinese weakness to detach Outer Mongolia from Chinese control. But the bitterest blow to Chinese pride was dealt at the Versailles Conference, which made the peace at the end of World War I. Technically the Chinese were among the victors, having declared war on Germany. Many Chinese believed in the Allies' slogans of democracy and self-determination for all peoples. Naively they expected the Versailles Conference to agree to abrogate all the unequal treaties the Western powers and Japan had imposed upon China in earlier days. Not only did the powers at Versailles fail to do anything of the sort, but—adding insult to injury— they denied China even the fruit of victory over Germany. Instead of returning to China the rights the defeated Germans had enjoyed in the Shantung Peninsula, the Versailles Conference handed them to Japan. The Chinese people were shocked by what they viewed as the betrayal of their legitimate aspirations. The resulting explosion in Peking took the form of a student riot on May 4, 1919. That riot gave birth to the "May 4th Movement," which many observers regard as the beginning of organized modern Chinese nationalism. A new generation had grown up since the defeat of the Boxers in 1900, and this new generation was more determined than ever that China should break the shackles of foreign control.

The leader to whom many of the young Chinese looked as a potential national savior was Sun Yat-sen, sometimes called the George Washington of China. Born near Canton in 1866, Sun became the intellectual leader of the generation of revolutionaries that toppled the Manchus. He received much of his schooling abroad, in Honolulu, and became a baptized Christian. Educated as a Western physician, he lived for long periods in the United States, Western Europe and Japan, devoting much of his time to propaganda for the overthrow of the Manchus and for the modernization of his native land. His prestige among the Chinese people was so high when the Manchus were ousted that he was named the first President of the Chinese Republic. However, he occupied the office very briefly, surrendering it to the man who held the military power at the time, the aforementioned Yuan Shih-kai.

Sun Yat-sen drew his basic ideas from many sources. He was influenced by such varied figures as the English economist John Stuart Mill, the American tax reformer Henry George and the leader of Russian Bolshevism, Vladimir Ilyich Lenin. Sun rejected Marxism and denied the need for class struggle in China. He believed in greater equality of land ownership among the peasants and Government ownership or regulation of certain industries. Essentially Sun represented the values of the Chinese middle class. In comparison with the theories Mao Tse-tung has imposed upon China, Sun's economic doctrines were mild indeed.

V

The Communist Conquest of China

KARL MARX and Friedrich Engels, the 19th-century founders of modern Communism, would have been greatly surprised had they lived to see the Communist conquest of China. They were men of the cities and looked to the industrial workers of the advanced capitalist countries to carry out the revolution they had predicted. They regarded the peasant masses with contempt and spoke in the Communist Manifesto of "the idiocy of rural life." Moreover, they were internationalists whose basic thinking was well reflected in the slogan "Workers of the World Unite."

How could the ideas of Marx and Engels win men's minds in China, a land composed over-whelmingly of peasants? How could those internationalist ideas triumph in a country caught up in the violent nationalism born of a century of humiliation at the hands of foreigners? Marx and Engels had been thinking of England, France, Germany and the United States when they wrote of Communism, not of remote China, so different from any society they had ever encountered.

Lenin and Mao Tse-tung, two of the prime shapers of the 20th century, made the adaptations of Marxism that enabled it to triumph in so unlikely a land as China. When Lenin seized power in Russia in 1917, he pioneered paths Mao was to follow. Russia, too, had many more peasants than workers, and it was Lenin's skillful wooing of the peasantry that spelled the difference between Communist victory and defeat. Lenin saw that Russia could be won only by forging an alliance of workers and peasants, and he did not hesitate in 1917 to advance even so un-Marxist a slogan as "All Land to the Peasants," a slogan that appealed to the private-property instincts of the peasantry and was diametrically opposed to Lenin's real goal of a socialized, collectivized agriculture. And it was Lenin who formed the concept of the Communist party as the instrument for the seizure of power. He insisted it be an army of fanatical revolutionaries working under what amounted to military discipline in organizing the masses.

Mao Tse-tung absorbed all these lessons and

then went further. He reshaped the image of Communism so that his countrymen could believe the Communists would serve China's national goals. No less important, he took a step beyond Lenin and based his revolutionary movement entirely on the peasantry, untroubled by the fact that this meant turning Marxism upside down. His inspiration for this move was the revolutionary ferment among Chinese peasants in the mid-nineteen-twenties. The deep impression a spontaneous peasant revolt in his native Hunan Province made on Mao is apparent in a report he wrote in 1926, a report that indicated the road he would later take to conquer China:

> The main targets of the peasants are the local bullies, the evil gentry and the lawless landlords. . . . In force and momentum, the attack is just like a tempest or a hurricane; those who submit to it survive, those who resist perish. As a result, the privileges the feudal landlords have enjoyed for thousands of years are shattered to pieces. . . .
>
> True, the peasants do in some ways "act unreasonably" in the countryside. . . . Turning everything upside down, they have even created a kind of terrorism. This is what some people call "going too far." . . . A revolution is not the same as inviting people to dinner or writing an essay or painting a picture

or embroidering a flower; it cannot be anything so refined, so calm and gentle. . . . A
revolution is an uprising, an act of violence
whereby one class overthrows the authority of
another. A rural revolution is a revolution in
which the peasantry overthrows the authority
of the feudal landlord class. If the peasants do
not use the maximum of their strength, they
can never overthrow the deeply rocted, age-
old authority of the landlords. The rural areas
must experience a great, fervent revolutionary
upsurge, which alone can arouse hundreds
and thousands of the people to form a great
force.

Perhaps Mao himself did not understand in 1926
what heresy he was uttering in putting such emphasis upon the peasants. But by 1938 he understood very well that he was a major innovator al-
tering Marxism sharply from its original Western
European and Russian forms. He showed his understanding then by sounding the call "to make
Marxism Chinese, to see to it that in every mani-
festation it bears a Chinese character—that is to
say, that it is applied according to China's special
characteristics." Still later the ideas he had called
"Chinese Marxism" were to be renamed "the
thought of Comrade Mao." This transformed

Marxism-Leninism now is for Chinese Communists what the Bible is for religious Christians and the Koran for devout Moslems. Outsiders may wonder whether Karl Marx, could he return to life, would be willing to claim any share of the parentage of "the thought of Comrade Mao."

Russia's Communist revolution took place in an era when Chinese intellectuals were examining Western ideas, trying to find a system that would suit China's 20th-century needs better than Confucianism. At Peking University and similar centers of learning, students and professors were debating the merits of Adam Smith, Bertrand Russell, John Dewey and other thinkers. Few had heard of Karl Marx, but news of Lenin's triumph stimulated interest in Marxism. The Communists who now ruled Russia dreamed of world revolution, but in 1918 and 1919 they were too busy fighting the civil war inside their country to do much about promoting Communism in China directly. There was, however, one weapon they could use: the weapon of propaganda. They employed it effectively by issuing a statement that took skillful advantage of Chinese resentment at the refusal of the great powers to give up their special privileges in China. Russia, the statement declared, would do precisely that, specifying:

The Soviet Government renounces the conquests made by the Czarist Government which deprived China of Manchuria and other areas. . . . The Soviet Government returns to the Chinese people without compensation of any kind the Chinese Eastern Railway, and all mining concessions, forestry and gold mines which were seized from them. . . . Not one Russian official, priest or missionary shall be able to interfere in Chinese affairs, and if he commits a crime, he should be subject to the justice of the local [Chinese] courts.

Later the Russians repudiated some of these promises. But to many Chinese this declaration seemed at the time to mean that the new Russia was the only country that really sympathized with China's just desires. Inevitably this made for sympathy with Lenin's new state and spurred interest in Communism's anti-imperialist preachments, thus helping the work of the agents Moscow sent to China in 1920 and afterward to help found and then direct a Chinese Communist party.

When it was established in 1921, the Chinese Communist party consisted of a small group of intellectuals who had been brought together by two Europeans sent into China by Communist International headquarters in Moscow. The moving spirits among the Chinese organizers were Chen Tu-hsiu and Li Ta-chao, professors of literature and history, respectively, at Peking University. One of their associates in founding the party was a young library clerk at the university who had had some experience in organizing workers and students in his native Hunan Province. The young man's name was Mao Tse-tung.

The intellectual founders of the Chinese Communist party knew little at that time about the formal doctrines of Marx or Lenin. What had won them over was Lenin's success in gaining power in Russia and the conviction that the Leninist road was the way to cure the weakness and sickness of China. Also, what was regarded as the Western betrayal of China at the Versailles Conference helped turn Chinese intellectuals toward Russia and Marxism-Leninism.

During the first decade of its existence the Chinese Communist party was essentially a pawn of the Soviet Union. The orders the Chinese Communists received from Moscow and obeyed reflected primarily the interests of the Soviet Union as interpreted by that country's post-Lenin ruler, Joseph Stalin.

As seen by Stalin in the early nineteen-twenties, the key force in divided and chaotic China was Sun Yat-sen's Kuomintang (National People's party), whose strength was in the south, around Canton.

Despite the middle-class nature of Sun's ideas, Stalin believed the Kuomintang could be used to unify China and lay the groundwork for an eventual Communist take-over. In January, 1923, Sun and agents of Moscow signed an agreement pledging Soviet aid to the Kuomintang. In addition, it was agreed that the Chinese Communists would enter the Kuomintang as individuals, though their party would retain its independent existence. The Chinese Communists promised they would obey Sun Yat-sen's orders and abide by Kuomintang policy while they were members of that organization.

Moscow's leaders were probably thinking of a Russian experience when they approved this agreement. In 1917 the overthrow of the Czar had been followed by formation of a moderate provisional government that was headed in its last months by Aleksandr F. Kerensky, who was ousted from power by Lenin. To the Russians Sun Yat-sen must have seemed a likely candidate for the post of the Chinese Kerensky. If Sun reunited China, Stalin presumably reasoned, he would in turn be overthrown and replaced by the Chinese Communist party. In short, the basic question was: Who would use whom? But the situation proved to be more complicated than Moscow may have imagined. Since many in the Chinese Communist party and the Kuomintang expected treachery from each other, their short-lived cooperation in the mid-nineteen-twenties took place in an atmosphere of mutual distrust.

Events moved swiftly after the 1923 agreement. Sun Yat-sen ordered his young aide, General Chiang Kai-shek, to Moscow to negotiate for military assistance. When Chiang returned he founded the Whampoa Military Academy to train officers for the Kuomintang's armies, financing the venture with three million rubles provided by the Soviet Union and filling key places in his academy with about 40 experienced Soviet officers. A Russian, Michael Borodin, arrived to become Sun's chief political adviser. Borodin had once been a school principal in Chicago and one of his key qualifications for his new task was the fact that he spoke English.

As the flow of Soviet personnel, money and arms increased, Borodin provided the leadership to revolutionize the Kuomintang, to turn it from a loose and inefficient organization into a highly centralized and effective political machine. Borodin's main premise was that the masses of China could be mobilized behind the Kuomintang if that organization promised to satisfy their grievances. The Chinese Communists were invaluable in the transformation of the Kuomintang, making available their organizational and propaganda skills. Thus strengthened militarily and politically, the Kuomintang armies under Chiang Kai-shek conquered much of China from the regional warlords during 1926–1928. Chiang's troops thus came closer to reunifying China than any other force had been able to do in more than a decade. But Sun Yat-sen, who had died in 1925, did not live to see the achievement.

Chiang wanted victory over the Chinese Communists as well as the warlords. In 1927 he ordered his armies to destroy the Marxist-Leninists, thus betraying the cooperation agreement. Some Chinese Communists had feared this might happen and had more than once protested Moscow's orders to cooperate with Chiang. But Stalin, confident that he could outwit the Chinese general, had rejected these protests. Moreover, at Stalin's orders, the Chinese Communists had concentrated on building their strength in China's great cities among industrial and transport workers. Thus, when Chiang struck, his enemies were concentrated in relatively few areas and were easy to find. Chiang attempted to drown Chinese Communism in the blood of its murdered supporters, an effort that almost succeeded. Stalin had been outsmarted, but the immediate cost was borne by the thousands of Chinese Communists who were killed or imprisoned and tortured. The pro-Moscow leaders of Chinese Communism made a few feeble attempts thereafter to win new centers of power by sponsoring armed uprisings in particular cities, but these were all crushed. As the nineteen-twenties ended, the once-powerful Chinese Communist party seemed to have been virtually destroyed and its dreams of proletarian revolution had never come to pass.

At this point in history, Mao Tse-tung gathered together a little group of miners, peasants and soldiers and climbed the steep slopes of Chingkanshan, the mountain that became his first stronghold. Communism's attempt to win China by concentrating on the proletariat had failed. Mao was determined to tap the revolutionary energy of the peasantry, and his success has shaped much of the history of the mid-20th century. Here is how he appeared to Henry R. Lieberman of *The New York Times* in the days before Communism conquered China. Mao, Mr. Lieberman wrote,

is not the kind of person one easily forgets. He is taller than the average Chinese, with pronounced cheekbones and unruly hair. He wears the simple clothes of the Chinese countryside.

An interview with Mao . . . is apt to last for hours, with Mao driving home his points with a precise, almost Jesuitical logic that winds through Marxian mazes and arrives at its intellectual destination with telling effect. He speaks the dialect of his native Hunan, and he has a ready sense of humor. . . .

Mao's past career indicates that he can be as ruthless as Generalissimo Chiang Kai-shek in carrying out a policy. In personality, however, they offer a strong contrast. The ascetic, patriarchal Generalissimo is a non-smoker and non-drinker. Mao, a chain smoker, has a lustier, fleshier personality.

Mao's social and economic theories seem to stem in part from his rural background, but in much larger part from the intellectual currents he encountered in his impressionable youth. It was a time of world-shaking events —the breakage of China's feudal bonds, World War I, the Russian Revolution—and the effects on Chinese students were profound.

Born to peasant parents in a village about 40 miles from Changsha, in the Hunan "rice bowl," Mao . . . was fond of his mother and detested his tyrannical father, who frequently beat him and made him study the classics instead of the historical romances he preferred. He entered the Hunan normal school in 1912, and received a teaching diploma in 1918. Despite his distaste for the . . . commentaries on the old sages, Mao learned enough Chinese so that he can still write acceptable classical poems.

After World War I, Mao came up to Peking to study at Peking University. Associates of the time remember him as an eager, vibrant country boy with long, wild, uncut hair and brilliant eyes. He used to sit in the library all day, a student without money, devouring book after book.

But Mao was a man of action as well as a student and thinker. It was this combination of qualities that determined his success. It is significant that his first published article, which appeared in 1917 when he was 23 years old, was titled "A Study of Athletics" and stressed the importance of hardening one's body for the struggles that lay ahead. Mao was set on being more than a bookish intellectual.

The formula by which he conquered China is easy to describe, but it was enormously difficult to carry out over almost a quarter of a century against large and well-equipped enemy forces. The essence of the formula was the building up of compact areas of Communist strength in the countryside, creating a complete governmental structure and effective military organization in each. This process continued until Mao's forces flowed in a victorious tide over all of Mainland China in the late nineteen-forties. Mao's recipe for winning peasant support was simple. It was to introduce the changes that the vast mass of poor peasants in each area wanted. Sometimes this meant killing landlords and rich moneylenders, canceling peasants' debts and rents and dividing the available land among the poor peasants. But in many places and at many times Mao's subordinates proceeded more cautiously in order to minimize the hostility of the richer peasants. In practice such caution meant that rents were lowered, not abolished, and that interest rates on peasants' debts were cut drastically, but the debts were not wiped out altogether. Mao taught his men to try to win the confidence and trust of the rural masses by treating poor peasants and small merchants fairly, by paying for the food and other goods they took and by introducing order and peace where there had been chaos and lawlessness. Mao himself set an example of simple living without luxury, an example that helped convince many that he and the Communist party really stood for the interests of the poor peasantry.

Yet if Mao had been only a political and economic organizer, he would never have triumphed. Time and again he had to meet the large and well-equipped Kuomintang armies that Chiang Kai-shek sent out to destroy Communist rule in different parts of the country. In fighting Chiang's armies Mao proved himself a great guerrilla warfare leader. Today the tactics he used against Chiang's troops and his writings on guerrilla warfare are military classics, studied by Communists and non-

Communists alike. He once summarized his strategy in this form:

> The enemy advances: we retreat.
> The enemy halts: we harass.
> The enemy tires: we attack.
> The enemy retreats: we pursue.

"Political power grows out of the barrel of a gun," Mao taught, always emphasizing that propaganda agitation and actual fighting must go hand in hand. Every weakness in the enemy's camp must be utilized, he told his followers, and every battle carefully planned. Guerrillas, he instructed his soldiers, must be like fish in the sea who cannot be distinguished from other fish when they congregate in large numbers. In other words, he told his troops who came from the peasantry that when faced by superior military force they must be prepared to hide among the peasantry so as to escape detection and death.

Mao taught his armies to get supplies by capturing them from the enemy and to replace their dead and wounded by winning over Chiang Kai-shek's soldiers captured in battle. In the late nineteen-forties, when Chiang's Kuomintang troops fought unsuccessfully—often with the latest American equipment at their disposal—to stop Mao's forces, Chinese Communist propagandists boasted truthfully of the immense quantities of American arms Mao's men had been able to take over and use themselves as they defeated enemy army after enemy army. Moreover, so skillful was Mao's propaganda that large numbers of Kuomintang troops defected to the Communists and fought against Chiang, their former leader.

Mao Tse-tung suffered defeats also before his final victory. His most severe test came in 1934–1935, the period during the celebrated Long March, a classic of courage, endurance and military and political skill which has won the admiration of Mao's friends and foes alike. In the early nineteen-thirties Chiang had made four unsuccessful efforts to destroy the Communist forces north and northeast of Canton. Each time Mao and his military commander, General Chu Teh, lured Chiang's men deep into Communist territory, split them up and defeated each Kuomintang formation by concentrating against it a larger mobile guerrilla group. In 1933, however, the Nationalist Government began its fifth and most carefully prepared anti-Communist drive, launching 700,000 soldiers, amply supplied with artillery and backed by an air force, against the territory held by Mao's guerrillas. After a year of hard and bloody fighting Mao felt he had no alternative but to escape from the enemy troops encircling his forces.

Thus began that epic of military history called

the Long March. Harried by Government troops, by shortages of food and medicine and by the often harsh climate, Mao's wandering army overcame incredible hardships. It climbed major mountain ranges, crossed turbulent rivers on perilous and primitive bridges and inched its way across great swamps. A year after he had started and 6,000 miles away from his starting point, Mao called a halt. He had arrived at the other end of his country, in northern Shensi Province in northwestern China. Fewer than one-third of the 100,000 men who had begun the Long March completed it; most had fallen victim to battle, hunger, cold or disease. But in this poverty-stricken region of China Mao created a new Communist area, set up his capital in Yenan and started all over. The expansion of Communist power that he began then ended only with his conquest of Mainland China.

Mao's political and military genius and his ability to inspire his troops with a willingness to fight were vital in determining his final victory. But three other factors also helped decide China's fate during the late nineteen-thirties and nineteen-forties.

From 1937 to 1945 the war against Japan drained Chinese energies and created conditions favorable to the growth of Communist strength. The war was the product of Japan's ambition to rule all of China. Japanese military victories early in the war (which began four years before Japan's attack on the United States at Pearl Harbor) brought most major Chinese cities under Tokyo's sway. In the face of this Japanese challenge, the alliance of the mid-nineteen-twenties was revived a decade later. With Moscow's blessing a new Communist-Kuomintang united front was formed. Simultaneously in the late nineteen-thirties a large amount of Soviet military aid was delivered to China to help stiffen Chiang's resistance to the Japanese. After the 1941 attack on Pearl Harbor, the United States became China's major supplier of weapons. But even while the war raged against the Japanese in the early nineteen-forties both Mao and Chiang regarded the struggle as one between themselves, and both had only contempt for their pledges to cooperate against the foreign foe. Mao substantially extended the area ruled by his forces during World War II, a dividend for his ability to win the minds and hearts of the peasants. Chiang's poorer performance is partly explained by an American observer's description of the Kuomintang army during the war:

The army rank and file were maltreated, ill-fed conscripts lacking the essential elements of military and political discipline. A large proportion of the Nationalist conscripts, often to be seen in Chinese wartime towns roped together to prevent escape, died even before reaching their assigned units. Thousands of others, deprived of basic medical care and even their rations by grafting superiors, died of neglect later. . . . The army's generalship was bad, and troop morale was worse. The Nationalist armies sat tight in defensive positions and hoarded their new American weapons for eventual use against the domestic opposition.

A second major factor that helped give Mao the edge over Chiang was the Soviet help he received after the Japanese surrender in 1945. Soviet troops had taken Manchuria from the Japanese and they helped the Chinese Communists seize northern Manchuria and build a major base there. From this base Mao mounted the final drive that obliterated Chiang Kai-shek's power on the mainland of China. The Soviet aid was relatively small compared with the assistance the United States gave the Nationalist forces during the middle and late nineteen-forties, but Mao's armies used their resources far more skillfully and effectively than did Chiang's.

Finally, during the civil war's last years, 1946–1949, when the Chinese Communists fought and won, the incompetence, corruption and lack of fighting spirit on the part of the Nationalists made their defeat inevitable. Inflation reigned in the cities ruled by Chiang Kai-shek, and the higher prices soared, the lower sank the morale of the middle-class forces that might otherwise have fought for the Kuomintang. In the countryside millions of peasants regarded Chiang as the defender of the oppressive landlords and moneylenders from whom the Communists promised to liberate them. As for the military factors involved, this comment by Major General David Barr, written in November, 1948, while he was the senior United States officer assisting Chiang Kai-shek, sums the situation up:

I am convinced that the military situation has deteriorated to the point where only the active participation of United States troops could effect a remedy. . . . Military matériel and economic aid in my opinion [are] less important to the salvation of China than other factors. No battle has been lost since my arrival due to lack of ammunition or of equipment. [The Kuomintang] military debacles in my opinion can all be attributed to the world's worst leadership and many other morale-destroying factors that can lead to a complete loss of will to fight. The complete ineptness of high military leaders and the widespread corruption and dishonesty throughout the armed forces could, in some measure, have been controlled and directed had the [necessary] authority and facilities been available. Chinese leaders lack the moral courage to issue and enforce an unpopular decision.

In these years Mao and his generals showed that they were more than able guerrilla leaders. Now they hurled their own vast armies against Kuomintang forces of similar size, and time and again it was the Communists who emerged victorious from these battles.

During the final months of the Chinese civil war in 1949 the Communists won victory after victory and took city after major city almost unopposed. When Mao Tse-tung proclaimed the formation of the Chinese People's Republic (the official name of Communist China) on October 1, 1949, his troops controlled almost all of Mainland China. For a time the remnants of the Nationalist regime found temporary refuge in western China. In December, 1949, however, the Nationalists fled the mainland altogether and took up residence on the island of Taiwan. For the first time since the Manchus, China again had a strong, effective central Government controlling virtually its entire territory. A new era of Chinese history had begun—the Communist era.

Now that more than 15 years have passed since the event, historical perspective suggests that the Communist victory over Chiang was probably inevitable. Chiang Kai-shek himself never showed the ability or the willingness to make the fundamental reforms in his government's policies or modes of operation needed to give it grass-roots strength among the masses of ordinary Chinese. In its last years on the mainland, his Kuomintang regime projected an image of ineffectiveness and corruption, gaining more and more the reputation of representing the interests of the landlords, the moneylenders and the merchants rather than those of the vast peasant majority. Mao Tse-tung and his Communists, on the other hand, succeeded in identifying themselves with the interests and desires of the majority, while their successes steadily projected an image of a new strong Chinese force that could better serve the national interest. Massive American military intervention might perhaps have staved off the Communist triumph and given Chiang another opportunity to reform his government and its policies. But in the years immediately following World War II, American women were in no mood to see their husbands, sons and sweethearts march off again to fight and possibly die in a distant land, and American men had had enough of fighting and dying in the war against Germany and Japan; they wanted to enjoy the benefits of postwar prosperity and peace. The view was undoubtedly short-sighted, but even now one can wonder how many hundreds of thousands or millions of American soldiers would have had to be sent to China to stem Mao Tse-tung's vast armies. In any event, it was not done.

But once Mainland China was under Communist rule, a myth quickly gained adherents among Americans and poisoned United States political life for years, playing a role in making possible the shameful period known as "McCarthyism," after the late Senator Joseph McCarthy, Republican, of Wisconsin. This myth held that the United States had somehow "lost" China because of treachery in high places. Some put the blame on Secretary of State Dean Acheson; others chose the Democratic party as a whole for a scapegoat. This was an escape into fantasy, because the United States never owned China, and in the last analysis China was conquered by Communists who are Chinese and who had relatively little Russian help. The United States tried to save Chiang Kai-shek and gave him billions of dollars' worth of aid. But he used it ineffectively, and much of the armament sent to his forces ended up in Communist hands.

It is a temptation for some Americans to believe that the United States is all-powerful and can do anything it wants to. On such an assumption, of course, it is easy to jump to the conclusion that China could have been "lost" only because of treachery. But those who take the trouble to study the facts know that the United States is not all-powerful and that many things happen in this world without our being able to control them. The fate of China in 1949 was fundamentally decided by the Chinese people, though they could hardly anticipate the high costs and many sacrifices that the decision would impose upon them.

VI

China Under Communist Rule: I

MORE THAN A DECADE and a half has passed since the Chinese People's Republic was established in 1949. During that time the 700 million Chinese have undergone a transformation without precedent in modern history. Even the agonies of the Soviet people in the Stalin era seem mild in comparison with the ordeal of the Chinese under Mao Tse-tung. China has in effect been turned into a vast laboratory for Mao's social, political and economic experiments. The Chinese people are the guinea pigs upon whom the experiments are performed. At the cost of great suffering and enormous effort a new China has been forged, a China reaching out for influence in many parts of the world, especially in Asia, Africa and Latin America. Still smarting from the humiliations that Western and Japanese imperialism inflicted upon their nation in the past, the leaders of today's China practice their own imperialism, seeking countries and peoples they can bend to their will.

One of the first things the Chinese Communists did after conquering Mainland China was to rid their country of almost all Western influence, though some countries that recognized the new regime—Britain, for example—retained small footholds in Peking. Very quickly Mao Tse-tung eliminated every vestige of the old privileges. The universities, hospitals and other institutions operated by foreign missionaries were taken over by the state. Western businesses were confiscated or otherwise forced to end their activities. The United States was particularly affected because its diplomats, correspondents, businessmen and missionaries were required to leave the country. Mao Tse-tung justified all this by saying he was following a policy of "leaning to one side," favoring the Communist camp in the world struggle. But to many Chinese it must have seemed that at long last China belonged to its people.

The anti-Western and other nationalistic moves of the new regime would not by themselves have enabled the Chinese Communist party to fasten its exclusive control upon the nation. The party claims somewhat more than 17 million members in the mid-nineteen-sixties, about 2.5 per cent of the population. In 1949, when the conquest of Mainland China was completed, party membership was less than one-quarter this size. How could and can such a comparative handful of people keep the vast multitudes of Chinese under their control?

The answer lies in that gigantic process of remaking human beings that Americans call "brainwashing" and the Chinese themselves call "ideological remolding." Superficially, at least, China has been turned into a nation of parrots resembling people, each faithfully squawking the party line of the moment and expressing gratitude to Comrade Mao for having shown the correct way to happiness. A. Doak Barnett, a veteran observer of the Chinese scene, has described the key method employed in washing men's brains clean of old ideas and filling them with approved new doctrines:

> The all-out assault on the minds of the people is carried on at the level of each individual Chinese with what is perhaps the most effective single technique used by the Communists—indoctrination through small "study groups." Millions of ordinary Chinese gather in groups of half a dozen to a dozen people— in factories, shops, schools and offices—to *hsueh hsi,* or "study," the ideology and policies of the regime. These groups, meeting reg-

ularly under leaders who report the thinking of every member to higher authorities, spend long hours discussing material transmitted to them by the party's propaganda agencies. The party line provides all the final answers in these discussions, but nevertheless the "study groups" examine in great detail all possible opinions on any ideological or political question in order to sweep away every obstacle to complete and unanimous agreement in support of the "correct" party line.

Criticism and self-criticism are the essence of this process. Each group member must participate actively, baring his inner self to the group and confessing past mistakes or lingering doubts. There is, as some Chinese have phrased it, no "freedom of silence" in these groups. No one can be passive, indifferent or neutral. Each member must stand up and be counted.

In this discussion process there is constant emotional and intellectual interaction among all members of a study group. Each person discovers that when group criticism centers on him, as it does at different times on all members, he is, in a sense, a minority of one whom all the rest try to convert to prove their loyalty. . . .

One former editor says: "You can't think

clearly, even if you think you can, when you are taking part in intensive 'study.' You instinctively realize that your real thoughts will some day pop out of your mouth and that therefore to be safe you either have to change your real thoughts or not think at all." A young girl just graduated from a university in Communist China reports, "Most students began to change after undergoing 'study.' That doesn't mean, however, that this 'change' was really 'conversion' in many cases. For most students there wasn't much to convert; they had no firm or well-developed ideology; they were an ideological blank. The change, therefore, was an acceptance of new ideas which filled a vacuum."

To make sure that those who have been brainwashed stay brainwashed, the regime goes to extraordinary lengths. Broadcasts, movies, newspapers, magazines and books are full of propaganda. So are the lessons one learns in school or college. Loudspeakers blare propaganda in the streets. Propaganda slogans are draped across buildings. Propaganda posters occupy every convenient spot. And to verify that the indoctrination has taken hold, every Chinese is kept under constant scrutiny —living in effect in a personal goldfish bowl. His neighbors are encouraged to keep an eye on him as he is urged to keep an eye on them. This is a busy-body's paradise in which every citizen knows that any word or action of his may bring him trouble if it is out of step with the party line. And the party claims the right to dictate in virtually all areas of life, from the kind of clothes one wears and the kind of work one does to the age at which one should marry and the socially desirable number of children a couple may produce.

Why did the Chinese people accept this totalitarian control over their lives and thoughts? The simplest answer is that after the defeat of the Kuomintang the Communists monopolized all organized physical force in the country and anyone who dared to try to oppose them publicly faced death, imprisonment or forced labor. Not long after they took power, moreover, the Communists crushed two groups that might have been expected to give them the most trouble, the landlords and the businessmen.

The landlords were disposed of largely between 1950 and 1952, when the Land Reform Law was carried out. The procedure employed was simple but effective. Into each Chinese village came a Land Reform Squad composed of Communist party members and trained sympathizers. The squad quickly got in touch with the poorest residents of the village, asked them about their complaints and told them about the iniquities of landlords in general and their own village's landlords in particular. When enough discontent and anger had been generated, complaint meetings were held. At these meetings carefully coached peasants got up and told how they had been robbed, exploited and otherwise victimized by the landlords, who were forced to be present, each wearing a dunce cap and badge identifying him as "Local Bully Landlord So and So." The aim of the gatherings was to whip up the villagers' hatred of their richer neighbors so they would be willing to demand that the landlords be shot or otherwise punished. Several meetings might be necessary in a particular village before passions were roused to a satisfactory pitch. Then the decision to kill a certain number of the landlords and spare others would be made. The land and other property of the landlords would be divided up among the peasants and the Land Reform Squad would move on to another village to repeat its performance. Some estimates hold that as many as two million landlords were killed during this campaign. Whatever the actual number, the landlord class was certainly wiped out economically by 1952.

Chinese businessmen—from rich factory owners to small shopkeepers—were originally courted by the Communists because Mao Tse-tung knew that China needed their technical and administrative talents. Even before his triumph he had sought to assure those he called the "national bourgeoisie"

—that is, patriotic businessmen—that they could live and work honorably under Communist rule. After the Communist victory over Chiang Kai-shek small political parties representing businessmen and shopkeepers were allowed to function and businessmen were encouraged to organize chambers of commerce and similar bodies. Early in 1952, however, the Government began what was called the "Five-Anti Campaign" aimed at bribery, tax evasion, theft of Government property, fraud and theft of Government economic secrets. The objective was complete terrorization of all businessmen. Employes were encouraged to testify publicly to the crimes their employers had supposedly committed. At "struggle meetings" businessmen were expected to accuse one another as well as to confess their own crimes. The tactics employed have been summarized by Mr. Barnett:

The manager of one large company was kept locked in his office for 17 days, while he was being interrogated and threatened; he confessed all his real and imagined sins several times, but his confessions were repeatedly rejected as unsatisfactory and incomplete. Another businessman was questioned continuously for three days and nights; the weather in Shanghai at this time was still wet and cold, and this man was clad only in his underwear for the whole period. Managerial personnel in another large company were handcuffed in their office for a long time when they denied that they were concealing large amounts of money. This type of humiliating and terrifying treatment was meted out to thousands of Chinese businessmen to force them to confess their "illegal earnings" and to make repayment for them to the government. It was all-out psychological warfare.

Terrorized by this campaign and often impoverished by the large fines levied upon them, Chinese businessmen were in no mood to resist the Government's suggestions that their factories or shops be turned into joint Government-private enterprises, with the former owners becoming in effect hired managers. Later, in the mid-nineteen-fifties, the Government "suggested" that businessmen turn many of these enterprises into completely Government-owned organizations. The businessmen themselves were offered compensation in the form of dividends that would be paid to them for five years or so. Well aware that the Government could simply confiscate their property if it wished, the businessmen handed it over with seeming enthusiasm. In some cities they held parades of "celebration," marching through the streets with bands playing to express their "joy" at being allowed to leave the capitalist class at last. The result was the end of significant private business in China; those businessmen whose talents and experience were deemed useful were kept on as state employes to run their former enterprises or were placed in other posts.

Besides brainwashing and terror, the Chinese Communists also used patriotism to strengthen their control in the early years of the nineteen-fifties. The resort to patriotism was made possible by the Korean War of 1950–1953. Despite the fact that Communist North Korea had invaded South Korea, Peking's propagandists told the Chinese people that this was the result of an evil American plot to conquer first North Korea and then China. The "Resist America—Aid Korea" movement was made a national campaign, especially after Chinese Communist troops in the guise of "volunteers" entered the Korean fighting. By rousing the Chinese people's fear of American attack, the campaign tended to rally them around the Government and made them submit to dictates and hardships they might have accepted less willingly in other circumstances.

From the beginning of their rule the Chinese Communists dreamed of quickly transforming their country into a major military and political power. They were well aware that in 1949 China was one of the poorest lands in the world and one of the least industrialized. In part this was the result of the destruction caused by the long war against Japan and the Mao vs. Chiang civil war that followed from 1945 to 1949. But even by 1952— after a good deal of recovery had been achieved from the worst disorganization of 1949—China's total annual production of steel (about 1.5 million tons) and of electricity (about seven billion kilowatt-hours) was equivalent to only two or three days' production of steel and electricity in the United States. In short, the China the Communists took over was an economic infant. Yet Mao dreamed even then of the day when his country would produce nuclear weapons, jet planes, missiles and complex machinery of all kinds, and have the power to be a decisive global force.

To achieve his goal, Mao had two assets. One was the virtually limitless manpower of China, a labor supply composed of people accustomed to working very hard for little beyond the bare needs of life. The second was the friendship of the Soviet Union, a country far more advanced scientifically and industrially than China. But in 1949 and 1950 the Soviet Union was still recovering from the terrible slaughter and property destruction of World War II. It was in no position to aid China on a very large scale. In early 1950 Stalin did give the Chinese a loan of $300 million, but this was a mere drop in the bucket. Any additional help Moscow provided would have to be paid for by Peking.

Mao did not flinch but set the Chinese masses to work. He sought to raise farm production to obtain more food and agricultural raw materials for his people and—no less important—to provide food, cotton, leather and similar goods that could be exported to Russia and other countries to pay for needed imports. Millions were conscripted to build dams and irrigation canals in an attempt to prevent destructive floods and bring life-giving water to parched fields. Great drives were mounted to kill off insects and birds that damaged crops. On the farms themselves the peasants who had received land in the anti-landlord campaign were encouraged—with more than a little compulsion behind the persuasion—to join "mutual aid teams" that engaged in joint cultivation of all the team members' land.

The increased agricultural production of the early and middle nineteen-fifties was used to finance the growing industrialization program. Old factories were rehabilitated and enlarged; new factories and mines were opened. Thousands of Soviet experts came to China to help train Chinese workers and to help design and build new power plants, manufacturing installations, railroads. Many of these new facilities were equipped with modern machinery from the Soviet Union. At the same time thousands of Chinese were sent to the Soviet Union. Some were workers sent to Soviet factories to learn new skills; others were students sent to Soviet universities to study physics, mathematics, chemistry, engineering, medicine, architecture and the other essentials of contemporary civilization. Everywhere in China the Soviet Union was held up as the example to be imitated. Millions of Chinese were encouraged to study the Russian language so they could read Russian textbooks and learn more easily from visiting Russian experts. In 1954 a group of Soviet leaders headed by Nikita S. Khrushchev visited Peking and promised to provide additional economic aid—again in the form of loans, not gifts—to build almost 200 industrial installations. In short, a massive transfusion of Soviet knowledge, machinery and trained manpower was pumped into China so it could industrialize as quickly as possible and emerge as a great power. Simultaneously China's Government speeded the opening of new schools and colleges, seeking to end mass illiteracy and equip as many Chinese as possible with the basic and advanced skills needed in an industrial society.

But even as Mao pushed industrialization he was aware that he would have to overcome the problem posed by more than 100 million land-owning peasant families. These families made up the bulk of the population. Their psychology was not that of workers but of small capitalists anxious to get richer. Even after the elimination of the landlords there were still rich peasants and poor peasants (the richest would, of course, be considered miserably poor by American standards). All disliked the heavy taxes the Government imposed upon them. Peasant resistance could threaten the regime's entire program and ultimately endanger Communist rule in China. Knowing this, Mao moved rapidly to end private farming and replace it with a system of collective farms.

The decisive battle against China's vast army of private farmers took place in the mid-nineteen-fifties when Mao ordered an intensive campaign to collectivize agriculture. All the regime's resources of persuasion and pressure were utilized with amazing results. Less than a year after Mao had issued his order it was announced that more than 110 million peasant families, 91.9 per cent of all farmers in the country, had formed over 700,000 collective farms. They had pooled their land, their livestock, their tools and other resources into larger units on which they had become workers paid according to the amount of work they performed. One concession softened this nearly complete socialization of agriculture: each collective-farm family was allowed to have a tiny plot of ground, a garden in which to grow vegetables and perhaps maintain a few chickens or a pig. The result of this vast change was that the peasants, who had originally been won over to support of the Communist party by the promise of land reform, were effectively deprived of the land that reform had given them. The Government hoped the change would increase farm production and agricultural tax revenues. The peasants, still mainly interested in their own well-being, adjusted to it by often concentrating on their own tiny garden plots and doing as little work as possible on the collectivized fields.

By the end of 1956, it is now clear, Mao and his colleagues were beginning to worry about their hold on the Chinese people. The Hungarian Revolution of October-November, 1956, and earlier disturbances in Poland had sounded a warning that popular revolts against Communist rule were possible. In China itself, despite the tremendous propaganda campaign and the Government's iron control, the many sacrifices imposed upon the population produced dissatisfaction that boiled to the surface in some places. Here is how Mao described the situation early in 1957 in a speech acknowledging that there were signs of serious trouble:

> Certain people in our country were delighted when the Hungarian events took place. They hoped that something similar would happen in China, that thousands upon thousands of people would demonstrate in the streets against the People's Government. . . .
>
> In 1956, small numbers of workers and students in certain places went on strike. The

immediate cause of these disturbances was the failure to satisfy certain of their demands for material benefits, of which some should and could be met, while others were out of place or excessive, and therefore could not be met for the time being. . . . In the same year, members of a small number of agricultural co-operatives also created disturbances, and the main causes were also bureaucracy on the part of the leadership and lack of educational work among the masses.

Mao argued in his speech that there could be conflicts—he called them "contradictions"—between different groups in a Communist-ruled country. To bring those conflicts into the open and reduce the tensions they created, he called for a policy to which he gave the slogan: "Let a hundred flowers bloom, let a hundred schools contend." This sounded initially like a signal for free speech and free debate. Mao said specifically that he believed even Marxism should be criticized. Such criticism would be beneficial, he held, because "Marxists need to steel and improve themselves and win new positions in the teeth of criticism and the storm and stress of struggle. Fighting against wrong ideas is like being vaccinated—a man develops greater immunity from disease after the vaccine takes effect."

For a few brief weeks in the spring of 1957, therefore, an unprecedented event took place. Critics and opponents of the regime were encouraged to speak up without immediate punishment; some of their speeches and statements were printed in the newspapers and read over the radio. As the days passed, every aspect of Communist party policy was attacked, from subservience to Moscow to economic mistakes. Some Chinese demanded that the party give up power while others called for killing all Communists. Students and professors denounced the "thought reform" movement and cried out for genuine freedom. One student summarized the population's economic grievances in these words:

When pork is unavailable and the price of vegetables has increased by 600 per cent in a year, it is difficult to convince the people that living standards have improved. The people have begun to lose confidence in the Central Committee [of the Communist party], and they say that, in certain ways, their situation is worse than it was in the days of the Kuomintang. . . .

It is more correct to say that the masses have divorced themselves from the party than to say that the party has divorced itself from the masses. . . . It is, of course, possible to

install machine guns to deal with trouble, but
what should be feared is that the machine
guns will be turned against those who first fire
them.

It is still unclear whether the whole "hundred
flowers" affair was planned as a trap for anti-
Communists foolish enough to expose themselves.
It may have been that Mao simply miscalculated
and never expected the volume of bitterly angry
complaints that welled up when free speech was
permitted. Whichever was the case, the period of
plain speaking was cut short. The Communist
party declared that the anti-Communist ideas were
really poisonous weeds that should not be confused
with beautiful flowers. An intensive campaign was
opened against "rightists" to punish those who had
revealed their anti-Communist sentiments and to
intimidate everyone suspected of sympathizing with
them.

The Communist party had enough force at its
command to carry out this campaign and to restore
the earlier monotonous uniformity of public expression. But the outside world had gotten a bril-
liantly illuminated look at the passions and hatreds
that burned in the minds of many Chinese who superficially gave every sign of being obedient and
loyal followers of Mao Tse-tung.

It is hard for outsiders to appreciate the great

courage that was required of the dissenters in China who spoke out in 1957. In eight short years Mao had created the most regimented, tightly controlled society the world has known in modern times, a society in which the individual has no rights and must not only obey his masters but also proclaim his boundless joy at being fortunate enough to live during the same era as Comrade Mao. A Chinese engineer who was in his native land at the time of the "hundred flowers" illustrates the regimentation of the people by telling of a prisoner who escaped from jail and then found it impossible to get food or shelter and so had no alternative but to return to his cell. The engineer notes the moral:

> In a society where everybody is assigned to a place, there is no danger of anyone running about freely. This is not because people are held in their places by force, but because if they break away there are no places where they can fit in. Everyone in China belongs to some organization: farm cooperative, factory, school, women's association, government office or at least a city block. Once his status is fixed, he cannot change it, only "the leadership" can. There is no place for hangers-on or loiterers. Everywhere—post office, bank, hotel, railway station, ration office, police sta-

tion—one is asked to show credentials. The mistake of the escaped prisoner was that he thought there was idle space in the society where he could hide, and he found out too late that outside the prison things were as much controlled as inside. What then was the point of escaping? The State decided that he belonged to the prison, so nobody wanted him anywhere except in the prison.

Since the Chinese Communist party has this kind of power over every Chinese, it is hardly surprising that in the aftermath of the "hundred flowers" outburst it was able to force many of those who had voiced criticisms to beg for forgiveness in the most humiliating fashion, abjectly proclaiming the error of their ways. Here, for example, is part of the public statement made by a leading critic, Chang Po-chun:

> I am an offender guilty of serious political mistakes. With your mercy I am permitted to stand before you and to use a few minutes to admit my mistakes and guilt and express my greatest determination to reform myself. . . . With all my heart I accept and give thanks for the denunciations and exposures by [those] who in the last few days brought to light my ugly and absurd words and actions. . . . I have a deep feeling that in reprimand-

ing and criticizing me the people of our country . . . are giving me a chance of rebirth. I
wish to express my heartfelt thanks once
again to the entire nation.

Having silenced the critics and dissenters, Mao
and his associates had to face the more difficult
problem posed by the conditions that had generated their outcry. It had been easy to dispose of the
landlords and the businessmen, but how was the
growing discontent of the masses to be overcome?
Everything was scarce in the China of 1957: food,
clothing, housing and other necessities—to say
nothing of luxuries. The population was increasing
rapidly, but there had been no adequate increase
in agricultural production. Industry was growing
(1957's steel production of almost six million tons,
for example, was about four times the output of the
early nineteen-fifties), but even this progress was
pitiful compared with China's needs and its leaders' ambitions. Was their country doomed to inch
along at this snail's pace, or was there some way of
rocketing ahead into a new era of unprecedented
power and plenty? The Chinese leaders believed
there was indeed a way. They called it the "Great
Leap Forward." It was to prove a disaster for
them.

VII

China Under Communist Rule: II

THE HISTORY of China since 1957 has been dominated by the consequences of the failure of the "Great Leap Forward." The most ambitious political, social and economic experiment any nation has ever attempted, it soon became in actuality the "Great Fall Backward." In the worst period of hardship, during 1960–1961, the very continuance of Communist rule over China was called into question by the discontent of the people. In the mid-nineteen-sixties the situation appears more stable as the result of substantial recovery from the low point of the early years of the decade.

While the basic motivation for Mao Tse-tung's reckless experiment in social engineering was the slow pace of China's progress up to 1957, it seems likely that two major developments that year helped encourage him to embark upon his tremendous gamble. One was the great increase in Soviet rocket strength revealed when Moscow shot aloft the first intercontinental ballistic missile in August, 1957, and then put its sputnik, the first artificial satellite, into orbit around the earth two months later. These Soviet triumphs must have bolstered Mao's confidence that Communism would conquer the world, while making him more impatient than ever with China's backwardness. A second factor that must have influenced Mao was a Soviet agreement in October, 1957, to help China become a nuclear power. Less than two years later, in June, 1959, Moscow reneged on this agreement and it was not until 1964 that China was able to construct its first atomic bomb. But in the heady, exciting days of late 1957 and early 1958 when he took the decision to order the "Great Leap Forward," Mao Tse-tung did not know that the Russians would go back on their promise.

This "leap" was to end China's backwardness and poverty within a few years by compelling the Chinese people to make a supreme effort to raise industrial and agricultural production more quickly than any other nation had managed to do. Mao Tse-tung appears to have thought for a time that he had discovered a short cut to utopia. Even the Soviet Union does not claim it has yet entered that period of abundance for all that Marxists call Communism. Soviet leaders claim only that their country has achieved Socialism, a state in which production is still inadequate to satisfy all needs and wants. But in late 1958 and early 1959 the Chinese Communists believed their people were working miracles of production never before witnessed on this planet. At the height of Peking's self-delusion in late 1958 a Chinese Communist party statement claimed that China would enter full Communism —implying an abundance no other nation had yet reached—in a few short years. If true, this claim meant that China would reach the Communist utopia ahead of the Soviet Union. Not until the middle of 1959 did Mao begin to realize that he had led his nation into economic disaster rather than into unprecedented prosperity. The Government retreated quickly, but not soon enough to spare the Chinese people the enormous deprivations and suffering of 1959–1962.

The "Great Leap Forward" was based upon two radical policies—one in industry and one in agriculture—that the Chinese Communist party imposed upon the country. The revolution attempted in industry went under the slogan "Walking on Two Legs." The revolution in agriculture revolved around a new and startling institution, the "people's communes."

By "walking on two legs" the Chinese Communists meant that their country should use two simultaneous means of industrialization. One was a continuation of the technique employed since 1950. It emphasized the construction of large, modern and expensive factories such as the giant An-shan Steel Plant, designed and equipped by the Soviet Union. But China could not rely solely upon such installations, the Communists held, because they took a long time to build and were few in number. So Mao and his colleagues decided on a "second leg," the utilization of China's enormous labor force to produce goods in hastily opened small and crude mines, factories and other establishments. The key element was the creation of tremendous numbers of primitive furnaces to make iron and steel, all using local ore, coal and other available resources in each area. At the height of this campaign it became a patriotic obligation of those who lived in every Chinese apartment house and worked in every Chinese factory to have a furnace in the backyard. In this period no Chinese village was complete without its furnace. All China was turning into a nation of metalmakers employing techniques similar to those used at the dawn of the Iron Age thousands of years ago. In July, 1958, a top Communist party leader, Chen Po-ta, reported that 800,000 small and medium-sized factories and mines were being constructed in the mass response to the "Walking on Two Legs" movement. He predicted that the small blast furnaces and converters being built would permit more iron and steel to be produced annually than had ever before been manufactured in China. The orgy of self-congratulation that these developments brought on reached its climax in April, 1959, when Premier Chou En-lai declared that Chinese industrial production had grown 65 per cent in 1958 alone, or almost as much as the increase for the whole five years between 1952 and 1957. In 1958, Chou claimed, production of pig iron, steel, electrical equipment, locomotives and motor vehicles had more than doubled. He gave the impression that by "walking on two legs" Chinese industry was actually moving ahead with the speed of a rocket.

The organizational transformation of China's rural areas during 1958 was even more profound. Here is how it was once enthusiastically described by the leaders of Chinese Communism:

In 1958 a new social organization, fresh as the morning sun, appeared above the broad horizon of East Asia. This was the large-scale people's commune in the rural areas of our country which combines industry, agriculture, trade, education and military affairs and in which government administration and commune management are integrated. . . . Within a few months, starting in the summer of

1958, all of the more than 740,000 agricultural collective farms in the country, in response to the enthusiastic demand of the mass of peasants, reorganized themselves into over 26,000 people's communes. Over 120 million households, or more than 99 per cent of all China's peasant households . . . have joined the people's communes.

The reality behind these words was an incredible effort to convert the 550 million peasants of China into a militarized labor force at the complete disposal of their rulers, with the peasants living a life resembling that of bees in a hive. There were variations between different communes, of course, but the general features common to all or most of them appear to have been the following:

An attempt was made to abolish private property and even at times to break up family life. Peasants were forced to surrender their private property and to give up the small garden plots they had been allowed to cultivate under the collective farm system. In many cases families were moved out of their homes and into dormitories. Meals had to be eaten in communal dining rooms and children had to be left in nurseries during the daytime so that millions of mothers could be freed for productive labor. In the early stages of the commune movement an effort seems to have been made to eliminate the use of money; commune members received free meals, free haircuts, free clothing and the like instead of cash wages that they could spend.

On a typical people's commune with, say, 10,000 or 12,000 workers a militarized labor system was usually inaugurated. Workers would be organized, often in groups of hundreds, and sent where needed to till the fields, build irrigation canals, construct dams, etc. Semi-military discipline in work was frequently supplemented by long hours of military drill, an activity justified by claims that the "American imperialists" were planning to attack China. The old intimate relationship between a farmer and his small plot of earth, the traditional basis of China's intensive agriculture, was ended. The people's communes were factories in the fields on a scale never before seen.

The typical commune attempted to embrace all the activities of the thousands or tens of thousands of people living on its territory. It operated factories, stores, dining halls, nurseries, "happy houses" for the elderly, medical facilities and a great variety of other installations. The goal was to make each commune a self-contained little world in which all the available workers, machinery and tools would be employed as the leaders thought fit, not as the individual laborers wanted. And since the commune managers were judged by production results, they had every incentive to work those under their command very hard for very long hours. Stories of communes whose members toiled 18 to 19 hours a day for weeks at a time were common during this period.

The aim of the commune system was probably best expressed by Mao Tse-tung: "The whole nation should be organized as militia, with the people's commune as the unit, so that the broad masses of the people become workers when entering factories, peasants when going to the field and soldiers when taking up arms." The all-purpose citizen, an automaton indistinguishable from his fellows, was the logical goal.

For the hundreds of millions herded into the communes and deprived of all their property, 1958 must have been a nightmare year of bewildering change and unending hard work. The impact must have been hardest upon the women who were taken away from their babies and kitchens and sent into the fields as manual laborers, expected to do the same work as men. And on those communes where an effort was made to end normal family life altogether by housing men and women in separate dormitories and permitting husbands and wives to see each other briefly only a few times a month, the blow to spirits and morale must have been shattering.

In the early fall of 1958 the Chinese Communist

leaders were apparently convinced that the communes were creating unprecedented progress in the countryside. They spoke of vast increases in food production and began predicting the quick achievement of full Communism. By December of 1958 some caution began to be expressed and the Chinese people began to be warned that the Communist utopia was not quite around the corner. But as late as April, 1959, Premier Chou En-lai boasted that "our achievements are phenomenal." He claimed that in 1958 production of grain, cotton and tobacco had more than doubled—an astounding feat. The industrial and agricultural gains claimed for 1958, if true, meant that economic miracles had been worked and China had been lifted to a level of prosperity it had never known in modern times.

The claims were not true, of course. What had happened was very simple. The leaders in Peking had put unbearable pressure on their subordinates throughout the country to achieve the hoped-for "Great Leap Forward." For those subordinates to increase production at the desired rate was impossible, but for them to report false statistics showing sensational gains was entirely possible and was done widely. Apparently even Mao Tse-tung was fooled. But the bubble finally burst in August, 1959, when a somewhat shamefaced Chou En-lai told the nation that checkups "show that the figures previously published on the 1958 agricultural output are a bit high." Grain production in 1958 had not been 375 million tons, as originally claimed, but only 250 million tons. Other commodities showed similar discrepancies. The 1958 "Great Leap Forward" had been largely a delusion.

Not long afterward it became clear that Communist China was in the grip of a major economic crisis. The Government began speaking of a terrible drought, unprecedented floods and other tremendous natural disasters that were said to be wreaking havoc across the country. If the reports could be believed, nature had entered into a conspiracy to frustrate Mao Tse-tung. Soon Peking began turning to Canada and other Western countries for hundreds of millions of dollars' worth of grain. Refugees from China began telling of hunger and famine. In 1960 and 1961 more and more reports leaked out of industrial production being cut, of great factories standing wholly or partly idle, of millions of people being sent out of the cities by the regime and back to the farms. Now the Government called on everyone to raise his own food as far as possible. The backyard iron and steel furnaces gave way to huge numbers of vegetable gardens. A complete blackout settled down on Chinese economic statistics. The boasts that had filled the air in 1958 and 1959 evaporated. Suddenly the talk was all of "readjustment" and the need for in-

creasing agricultural output. The bright dream of a
Communist utopia had turned into the nightmarish
reality of a desperate fight against mass starvation.

What went wrong? The official explanation
blames two factors: an unprecedented succession
of natural disasters from 1959 to 1961 or 1962, and
the "treachery" of the Soviet Union, which withdrew many hundreds of its technicians from China
in the summer of 1960, dealing a body blow to
Mao Tse-tung's whole industrialization program.

A less biased view must give a large share of the
blame to Mao, the Communist party he heads and
the disastrous policies they imposed upon the Chinese people. The backyard furnace movement was
a failure, for the poor-quality iron and steel produced had little if any utility. But tens of millions of
man-days were wasted tending the furnaces. Much
more important were the blunders in agriculture.
In the communes the peasants lost most of their
former incentive. After all, the average peasant
must have asked himself, why should he work hard
on strange land, especially when the man who
shirked work ate the same meal at the communal
dining room as the man who exerted himself?
Moreover, the giant communes were plagued by
fantastic mismanagement. Many of the officials
who ran them were ignorant of farming methods
and had no experience supervising thousands of
people.

The essence of the matter was probably this: Chinese agriculture had fed vast numbers of people over the centuries because each peasant tended his small plot with loving care and knew from his own and his ancestors' long experience how best to cultivate and irrigate his crops to obtain the highest possible yield. All this knowledge and all this devotion to the soil were heedlessly tossed aside in the commune movement. To make things worse, the ambitious irrigation systems and dams built by armies of impressed peasants often hurt rather than helped agriculture because they were constructed under the orders of men who were ignorant of local conditions and incapable of taking every important factor into account. Unwise irrigation made large areas swampy or poisoned them with alkaline substances. Dams erected in the wrong places contributed to floods when the rains came.

Little of this could be admitted publicly, of course, because the legend of Mao Tse-tung's wisdom and infallibility had to be preserved. But as the magnitude of the crisis became plain in 1960 and afterward, the Government did take steps. The people's communes, for example, were dissolved in effect, though not in name, and agriculture was returned to what amounted to the old collective farm system. The peasant was allowed to cultivate his garden plot again and to raise his few chickens or a pig or two. Incentives were restored so that the hard-working peasant earned more than his lazy neighbor.

In the hungry years of the early nineteen-sixties the Chinese Communist regime was put to a severe test. It feared a mass uprising. Secret Chinese documents that have reached the West reveal that the rulers in Peking even became nervous about the continuing loyalty of the army. The typical Chinese soldier is still a country boy with many close ties to his native village. He could hardly be indifferent to letters from his family and friends telling of the hardships they were suffering back home. The Chinese leaders made sure the army was adequately fed, but for many months they worried whether this would be adequate to insure its loyalty.

These fears help explain the Communists' decision to begin a massive campaign to cut the country's birth rate and thus reduce the number of new mouths to be fed. Available statistics suggest that in the nineteen-fifties China's population may have been increasing each year by 12 to 15 million people. As the Communists introduced modern knowledge about sanitation throughout the country, as they trained doctors and nurses, as their factories started to produce more medicines, the death rate tended to decline. But if the death rate fell while the birth rate remained high, the population increase would accelerate rapidly. The outlook was appalling. United Nations statisticians, for example, have estimated that China's population will zoom from the 700 million of 1960 to a billion by 1980 and then to 1.6 billion by the year 2000. How could an already hungry and poverty-stricken China hope to feed, clothe and house these additional multitudes? The birth rate must be cut to prevent utter catastrophe, the rulers in Peking decided.

In typical fashion Mao Tse-tung and his colleagues went all out in the effort to slow down the population increase. Men who consented to have themselves sterilized so they could not become fathers were given national publicity and hailed as heroes. The not-very-subtle suggestion was that others should follow their example. Birth-control information and materials were made widely available. A campaign was even launched against early marriage, a campaign that at times assumed the aspects of an anti-love movement. Here is the way a French correspondent in Peking, Jacques Marcuse, describes a typical incident in this campaign:

Comrade Wang (male) called some weeks ago on the local registrar of marriages in the suburb of Peking where he lives and informed the registrar of his intention to marry Comrade Yu (female). Asked why, he gave the ludicrous answer: "Because we are in love."

He was then carefully cross-examined about

his and the young woman's background and told finally that they were both too young (respectively 24 and 22) to contemplate matrimony, and that love was no excuse—and certainly no substitute—for "political affinities."

"Since you are bound to know that it is the policy of the Government and of the Communist party to discourage early marriages for reasons which have been carefully and repeatedly explained," said the registrar, "are we to assume that your application is essentially intended to defy this policy and to show your disapproval of it?" He went on to suggest that if Comrade Wang could not reply with a clear negative, he had better think things over. "If you don't change your mind, come and see us again."

Comrade Wang beat a somewhat shamefaced retreat. Comrade Yu took fright and broke off the engagement.

But what about couples already married? Mr. Marcuse describes another technique that discourages many of them from having children:

Married couples are often separated. I know of wives whose husbands are employed in Shanghai and who themselves work in factories as far away as Sian. They meet once a year during their two-week vacations, and traveling expenses are paid by the state. Their children, if any, are taken care of in Government kindergartens and later in Government boarding schools.

To many Americans, life in China—with its poverty, its regimentation and thought control, its lack of individual freedom and its resemblance to a beehive or anthill existence—seems almost too horrible to contemplate. Why do the Chinese put up with it?

Part of the answer lies in the constant diet of propaganda and the fact that the Government controls all organized force. Important as these factors are, however, they do not tell the whole story. It must be remembered that the Chinese are no strangers to poverty and hardship. They accept their lot more philosophically than might a people accustomed to a better life. Beyond this, moreover, many Chinese believe that the Communist regime has bettered their existence and given them new hope.

They point, for example, to the vast expansion of education throughout the country. In a land where education was once the near monopoly of a small group, it is no mean achievement that more than 100 million youngsters now attend primary or secondary school. There are tens of thousands of bright and talented young Chinese whose ancestors were illiterate and who would themselves have been

illiterate had they been born into the old order. Today they look forward to becoming scientists, engineers, teachers and the like. There is an inex-
haustible number of jobs for those with the requisite
training, knowledge, ambition and energy. The
new opportunities are open to women as well as
men. This has truly revolutionary implications for
China, in whose ancient culture the inferiority and
subservience of women were taken for granted.

Nor would it be wise to ignore the extent to
which the Communist regime has brought some of
the gifts of science and technology to millions of its
people. We have already mentioned the great expansion of medical care. The truck, the automobile,
the radio, the motion picture, the book and the tele-
phone are now far more a part of the Chinese scene
than ever before, though of course they are far
scarcer than in the United States. No doubt many
of these advances would have occurred regardless
of who ruled China during the nineteen-fifties and
nineteen-sixties. But since they are the rulers, the
Chinese Communists get the credit in the minds of
many of their people.

The Communist ideology also plays a key role
in the Peking regime's hold on the nation. This
ideology presents a picture of a better world in the
future, implying that present-day sacrifices are
worthwhile because they help attain the brighter tomorrow. The hopes thus generated help make cur-

rent hardships bearable. Moreover, the Chinese Communist ideology glorifies the common man and depicts him as the all-powerful shaper of history. This is flattery indeed in a country where for thousands of years the common man was considered of no importance, fit only to work, to pay taxes, to fight in war and to father a new generation of toilers for tomorrow. Perhaps the most remarkable expression of the new glorification of the common man has been the "Love and Emulate Lei Feng" movement that swept over China in 1963 and 1964.

Lei Feng is said to have been a soldier who died in an accident at the age of 22. Totally unknown and unsung during his lifetime, he became a national hero after his death, the personification of all Marxist-Leninist virtues and the man all Chinese were exhorted to imitate. Jacques Marcuse has described the Lei Feng movement in these words:

> Throughout the country, tens of thousands of mass meetings were held to extol Lei Feng, chiefly for the benefit of the younger generation; excerpts from his diaries were published and broadcast, tales of Lei Feng were told before village audiences by professional storytellers, and stage and screen plays were written and produced in which he appeared as the central character, an example to all.

The very figure of Lei Feng began to take

shape. One could see him in one's mind's eye, always cheerful, helpful and busy, a totally dedicated Red pioneer who never wasted one minute of the day, generous with whatever money he had, but never spending any on himself, frugal in all things, yet resourceful to the point of hitting upon the one novel and economical idea that circumstances called for —e.g., patching the torn seat of his trousers with the lining of his military cap. Lei Feng was always kind and gentle, bustling about helping others, urging others to find their inspiration in the teachings of Chairman Mao; he was scornful of all creature comforts, clean of heart, mind and body, in love only with the party, its leader, China and the oppressed masses of the world—half Galahad, half Boy Scout. "I can give up everything of myself," he is supposed to have written, "but I cannot betray party, class or revolutionary cause."

Finally, Chinese Communism has sought to strengthen its rule by wrapping itself in the flag— appealing to the patriotism of the Chinese people and portraying Mao Tse-tung as the leader who will restore to China its ancient glory and power. Mao appears before his subjects as the man who threw the arrogant foreigners out. Peking's propaganda holds that he returned China to the Chinese, not only getting rid of American, British, French and Japanese influence, but also freeing the country from Russia's tentacles.

It is no accident that Communist China began to quarrel publicly with the Soviet Union during the bad years of the early nineteen-sixties. It was precisely at this time that Mao most needed to prove he was for China above all else, that he was not a puppet of Moscow. When the Russians withdrew their experts from China in the summer of 1960 Mao turned that blow into an asset by calling upon his people to show "self-reliance," implying that China would not bow to Soviet dictation regardless of what hardships had to be borne. Thus Mao sought to equate opposition to his rule with lack of patriotism. The Chinese attack on India in 1962 fits into the same pattern, for here Mao was able again to portray himself as the patriot. India, the Chinese people were told, was seeking to steal land that belonged to China and this could not be allowed.

But China's greatest enemy, it has been dinned into the Chinese people, is the United States. In Peking's propaganda the United States represents all evil—the country that has "stolen" Taiwan from China and will not return it, the country that allegedly wishes to attack China and enslave its people, the very incarnation of what Mao calls "capitalist imperialism." In effect the theme of all this is that China must be strengthened so that the evil

designs of the United States will be frustrated—
otherwise China will again suffer the national humiliation and weakness of the century before 1950.
It is significant that at the height of Mao's quarrel
with Khrushchev before the latter's ouster in October, 1964, the basic Chinese accusation was that
Khrushchev had allied the Soviet Union with the
United States in a plot to put China and the rest of
the world under the joint domination of Moscow
and Washington.

It is against this background that the political
and psychological importance of Communist China's explosion of an atomic bomb in October, 1964,
should be assessed. This was the greatest Chinese
technological accomplishment in centuries, proof
that Mao Tse-tung was progressing toward his goal
of making China a powerful modern nation. Whatever the earlier failures in industry and agriculture,
this was truly a "great leap forward" in Chinese
military technology. And Peking's propaganda fully
exploited the feat to encourage every Chinese to
feel proud of his country and its Communist regime. After all, what emperor before Mao Tse-tung
had ever had such a mighty weapon at his command?

Yet how could backward, poverty-stricken
China have produced an atomic bomb? Doesn't
that accomplishment suggest a greater economic
advance than has been implied by this author's re-

cital of the failures of the industrial and agricultural "Great Leap Forward"?

I do not minimize the importance of Peking's
bomb if I note that it largely represents the product
of a virtually isolated island of top-flight science in
the great ocean of Chinese backwardness. China
has had for several decades a relatively small group
of first-rate scientists and engineers. The older
men among them were educated in the West; the
younger ones have been trained in China and the
Soviet Union since the Communists took over. Peking put the highest priority on construction of an
atomic bomb. The nation's best scientific and technological manpower was assigned to the job, and
expense was no object. But, even so, the bomb was
not constructed until more than 15 years after
Communist China came into being. The United
States, Britain, France and the Soviet Union all produced atomic bombs ahead of China. India, Japan
and most European countries could have done so
had they wished. Peking's feat, in short, is not
proof of the "excellence" of the Chinese Communist
system. It simply proves once again that if a government has complete command over the people
and other resources of a large country it can con-
centrate those resources upon one or two high-
priority objectives and attain them. Stalin demonstrated this when, despite the great poverty of the
Soviet Union immediately after World War II, he

concentrated his resources on making atomic bombs and exploded his first one in 1949. In this, as in other matters, Mao has followed the example of Stalin. The people of China have borne the cost as the people of the Soviet Union earlier paid the price of carrying out Stalin's decisions.

Undoubtedly the atomic bomb has given Mao's regime great prestige among the Chinese people, but that prestige is likely to be only a temporary phenomenon. After the Chinese have become accustomed to nuclear weapons they will still want to live better and to have more freedom than they enjoy under their current rulers. Even today Mao's subjects try every trick possible to serve their own interests rather than those of the state. A revealing insight was provided by Mao himself when he spoke to the American writer Edgar Snow early in 1965. It is impossible to know how many people there are in China, Mao insisted, because they cheat. When a person dies his relatives often try to hide the fact of his death so they can continue to use his ration coupons to obtain the food and clothing he would have been entitled to. Peasants attempt to conceal some of their produce from the state so they can eat it themselves or sell it at high prices in nearby towns.

Mao Tse-tung worries most about the young people, the generation that has come to maturity since his triumph in 1949. A Chinese less than 25 years of age has few memories or none at all of what life was like before the Communist conquest. He tends to take the Communists' achievements for granted and to want further progress. And precisely because more and more young Chinese now have some education, their horizons are broader and their desires are more urgent than those of their less-educated parents. The pressure for a better life is likely to increase in the years ahead, especially as the Chinese people learn more about the outside world from which they have been artificially cut off for so many years.

VIII

The Sino-Soviet Split

ON MARCH 6, 1965, something strange happened in Peking: a protest demonstration by about 400 Chinese students in front of the Soviet Embassy. The immediate cause was the brutality Soviet police had shown two days earlier against Chinese students who tried to storm the United States Embassy in Moscow to protest American bombing of North Vietnam. More fundamentally, however, the demonstration in Peking was another expression of the Sino-Soviet conflict, the most important international political development of the first half of the nineteen-sixties.

It took a long time for Americans to come to believe that there really is a Chinese-Russian split. During the nineteen-fifties most Americans assumed that all Communists were united in pursuit of one objective: the destruction of the non-Communist world. Superficially, at least, there was much evidence to support this view. In the nineteen-fifties the Chinese and the Russians never tired of proclaiming their "eternal friendship," their "comradely cooperation" and the like. Even after the struggle between Moscow and Peking came out into the open in the early nineteen-sixties Americans remained skeptical that the two Communist giants could really be at each other's throats. This skepticism was expressed as recently as January, 1963, by President Kennedy. At that time he contended that the Soviet Union and China were merely differing on how best to "bury" the United States. This, he declared, was a quarrel from which Americans could take little comfort. Yet less than six months later the actions of the Kennedy Administration showed clearly that it regarded the Sino-Soviet split as a most important reality.

In retrospect it is evident that the American hesitancy to acknowledge the fact of the rift was based on an exaggerated belief in the unifying power of Communist ideology and an inadequate appreciation of the long-standing national and even racial differences between the Russians and Chinese. Very few Americans, for example, had any idea of how bitter and frequent Russian-Chinese conflicts have been over the centuries. Actually, the remarkable thing is that Moscow and Peking were able to maintain the appearance of friendship as long as they did. It was implicit in their background that even though both claimed allegiance to Marxism-Leninism they should become rivals and finally enemies.

We have noted earlier the many examples of Soviet-Chinese cooperation during the nineteen-fifties. Stalin gave China a loan of $300 million in 1950, and additional credits for Chinese industrialization followed. Thousands of Chinese students were sent to study at Soviet schools or factories and thousands of Soviet specialists came to China to help build new factories, mines and power stations. During the Korean War of 1950–1953 Chinese troops were largely equipped with Soviet weapons and depended upon Soviet oil, ammunition and other supplies. All during the nineteen-fifties the Soviet Union was both China's biggest customer and its main source of machinery and other needed items.

Yet even in this period sharp-eyed observers could detect signs of tension between Moscow and Peking. They noted, for instance, that before 1955 the Chinese had eased the Russians out of their special position in Manchuria. The Russians gave up their half-ownership of the Chinese Eastern Railroad and removed their troops from the cities of Port Arthur and Dairen—in short, the Russian special privileges in China were ended more slowly and more politely, but eventually no less thoroughly, than those of the British or Americans or Japanese. In the Korean War, Soviet troops did not come to the aid of the North Korean and Chinese forces and it later became known that supplies Moscow provided for the Chinese troops during the fighting had not been a gift but a loan that the Soviet Union expected Peking to repay. Then, in 1958, the Russians made it abundantly clear that they disagreed with China's "Great Leap Forward." In fact, Khrushchev told Senator Hubert Humphrey, who was later to become our Vice President, that the Russians had tried communes long ago and knew them to be useless. He was probably expressing resentment at the fact that Peking's propaganda at the time was hinting that China would reach full Communism ahead of the Soviet Union, thus implying that the Chinese were better and more successful Communists than the Russians. Finally, in 1959 Peking was extremely cool toward Khrushchev's visit to the United States at President Eisenhower's invitation. So even from the public evidence there was good reason to suspect that the claims of "eternal Soviet-Chinese friendship" and the tributes to the 1950 Soviet-Chinese amity treaty concealed more than a little friction between the two nations.

Disclosures by both Moscow and Peking these last few years have made it clear how very great that friction really was. Its roots, moreover, lie deep in the past. Perhaps I may be pardoned here if I use my 1964 book, *Tsars, Mandarins and Commissars: A History of Chinese-Russian Relations,* as the basis for a brief summary of the historical background.

Russia and China began the modern phase of their relations in the sixteen-fifties when the Russians, advancing toward the Pacific along the Amur River Valley, met Chinese subjects already living there. The struggle that began with that meeting three centuries ago has not yet ended. Using armed force and diplomatic trickery, the Russians over the long years seized from the Chinese all of what is now the Soviet Far East and much of what is now Soviet Central Asia, an area well over a half-million square miles. Taking advantage of China's weakness at the time of the fall of the Manchu Dynasty, the Russians turned Outer Mongolia into a Russian protectorate. The Chinese regained control over this area during World War I, but in the early nineteen-twenties the Soviet Union captured real power there. In Manchuria a Russian push threatened many times to turn that vast segment of China into a Russian colony, and as late as 1929 pitched battles for control of parts of Manchuria took place between Chinese and Soviet troops. There is a century of history behind the Russian and then the Soviet attempt to penetrate and seize Sinkiang Province in northwestern China. In short, the record shows that the Russians have, in the long run, been the most successful of the imperialists who preyed on China. A large part of the Soviet Union today is territory the Chinese feel was stolen from them in the 19th century and earlier, when China was weak and Russia strong.

Adding to Peking's bitterness is the history of the Chinese Communist party in the nineteen-twenties. Stalin then treated that party as his creature, naming and removing its leaders as he pleased. It was his bad advice that caused the party to get into a position where Chiang Kai-shek in 1927 was able to crush it almost completely by striking at the centers of Communist strength in the great cities. Only after the Chinese Communists had been driven into the rural areas, where communication with Moscow was bad or nonexistent, and had turned to Mao Tse-tung for leadership did they begin to build the strength that brought victory. We now know that at the end of World War II Stalin sought to dissuade the Chinese Communists from trying immediately to overthrow Chiang. It was only by disobeying Stalin's advice that Mao was able to fashion the strategy that won.

There must have been resentment and suspicion on both sides when Stalin and Mao met in December, 1949, shortly after Mao's victory. But the first clash to which both sides admit came in 1954, when Khrushchev and other Soviet leaders visited

Peking. Mao apparently demanded that the Russians return Outer Mongolia to China, a demand the men from Moscow rejected on the contention that Mongolia was an independent country. Tension mounted. In 1956 the Chinese encouraged the Poles and the Hungarians to try to gain greater independence from Moscow. A year later the Russians tried to buy Chinese support by promising to help Peking become a nuclear power, but in less than two years Moscow decided it had made a mistake and renounced its pledge. By 1960 the bad feeling between the two nations had exploded into outright enmity. The Soviet Union recalled all its experts who had been helping to build up China's industrial and military strength. This move came just when Peking was struggling with the harsh setbacks in agricultural production that followed the enormous failure of the people's communes. The removal of these Soviet experts dealt the Chinese a severe economic blow at the time they could least afford it.

Since then the Soviet-Chinese struggle has expanded and it has split the international Communist movement into three major camps: pro-Soviet, pro-Chinese and neutral. Many countries now have two Communist parties, one pro-Moscow and the other pro-Peking. The Chinese have the support of some of the most important parties, including those that rule Albania, North Korea and North Vietnam as well as the largest Communist party in the non-Communist world, Indonesia's. The Communist parties of Japan and New Zealand also back Peking.

Essentially the struggle between the Soviet Union and China is a fight for power. Each wishes to be the sole ruler of the world Communist movement. The Chinese also want the Russians to return the more than 500,000 square miles of Soviet territory that once belonged to China. Naturally neither side admits that its actions stem from selfish motives. Each claims to represent the only true variety of Marxism-Leninism and accuses the other of betraying the genuine Communist cause. In the debate, moreover, each distorts the other's position. Their arguments can be briefly summarized.

The Soviet stand—which was stated most clearly while Khrushchev was Premier and his country's Communist party chief—boils down to these main points: In the present era, when there are hydrogen bombs that could destroy most of the world's people, Communism must emphasize peaceful coexistence—that is, economic and political competition with capitalism—and seek to avoid a suicidal global war. The Chinese leaders are fanatics who would gladly see a nuclear conflict, since they are confident that enough of China's immense population would survive so that Peking could rule the world. The Chinese have abandoned

Marx's teachings about the opposition of labor and capital and have replaced it with a racist doctrine that seeks to set the nonwhite people of Asia, Africa and Latin America against the white people of the Soviet Union, Europe and North America. Mao Tse-tung is a dictator worshiped as a god in a way that makes a mockery of real Communist beliefs. His goal is to be the overlord of the entire planet.

The Chinese argument—directed first against Khrushchev and then against his successors, who are accused of carrying on "Khrushchevism without Khrushchev"—rests on these assertions: The Soviet leaders have abandoned the cause of Communist take-overs through revolutions and seek instead an alliance with the United States for joint Soviet-American rule over the world. Moscow's charges that Peking has adopted a racist doctrine are really intended to cover up the fact that the Russians want to set the white people against the nonwhite people. Soviet talk about the danger of a nuclear holocaust is primarily intended to discourage revolution; armed revolutions can be carried out without causing atomic war. Inside the Soviet Union the way is being paved for a return to capitalism. What is needed is the ouster of the present Soviet leaders and their replacement by true Communists who will really seek to aid the cause of world Communist revolution.

In the Moscow-Peking struggle many tactics

have been employed. There is reason to believe the Soviet Union supported a faction of the Chinese leadership that sought to remove Mao in 1959. Conversely, when a purged Soviet leader, Vyacheslav M. Molotov, tried to challenge Khrushchev before the Soviet Communist party Congress in 1961, he advanced an alternative platform that embodied much of the Chinese Communist program, implying he had Peking's support. The Chinese have sought with frequent success to bar the Russians from meetings of African and Asian nations on the ground that the Soviet Union is really a European power which has no place in Asia and should surrender its vast Asian territory. The catalogue of areas in which the struggle is taking place could be greatly expanded.

This split in Communism has naturally had many important repercussions, opening possibilities for American diplomacy that did not previously exist. One result was the 1963 Soviet-American-British agreement banning nuclear weapons tests in the atmosphere, in outer space and under water. The Chinese opposed this accord, declaring that it was aimed at preventing them and other nations from developing their own nuclear bombs. Paris, which wants to strengthen French nuclear power by developing hydrogen as well as atomic bombs, agreed with Peking, opposed the treaty and in effect formed a Franco-Chinese alliance in favor of a continued nuclear arms race. The decision of the United States early in 1965 to use its planes to attack North Vietnam was undoubtedly based in part upon the calculation that since North Vietnam supports China, the Soviet Union would be reluctant to come to North Vietnam's aid by entering that war itself.

From February to at least late July, 1965, the United States calculation proved correct. Though Moscow and Peking both denounced the American air attacks on North Vietnam, they did not join strategy or forces against the United States. During this period, in fact, the Chinese published a bitter attack against the men who had succeeded Khrushchev. Communist officials in Moscow, moreover, spread the report that the Chinese were blocking the rail shipment of Soviet military supplies to North Vietnam over China's territory.

The tension over North Vietnam between the two Communist giants reflected the fact that they are rivals for influence and power in Southeast Asia as well as elsewhere. The Chinese would like to force the United States out of Vietnam, end its influence in Thailand and so on in order to make China the dominant power in that part of the world. Peking had and has no desire to tolerate Soviet influence in this area. During the final months of Khrushchev's rule in 1964 there were signs that Moscow was willing to abandon its own ambitions in Southeast

Asia and let the Chinese and the United States battle it out for primacy there. But when Soviet Premier Kosygin visited North Vietnam in February, 1965, he was clearly asserting continued Russian interest in the area. The repeated reports that North Vietnam's Communists are divided into pro-Soviet and pro-Chinese factions is another reminder of the continuing struggle for power between the two Communist giants.

Looking ahead, it seems unlikely that the Sino-Soviet split can be fully healed in the foreseeable future. The Chinese have scored numerous and impressive political and ideological victories against the Russians since 1960 and appear confident they can make more gains by continuing to oppose Moscow. The Soviet leaders have tacitly recognized their setbacks by trying to conciliate the Chinese, who have refused to be appeased short of Moscow's unconditional surrender. All this could change, of course, after Mao Tse-tung's death, but the basic factors of national rivalry, racial animosity and the enormous difference in living standards between the two countries are powerful forces dividing them, no matter who their leaders are. Historically, culturally and emotionally the Russians have far more in common with the people of Europe and the United States than they have with the Chinese and other Asians. This fundamental fact is likely to be much more important in the years ahead than the ideals of Communism. Those ideals have provided but a flimsy and inadequate basis for Soviet-Chinese unity in the past; they are unlikely to provide any stronger basis in the future.

IX

The "Second China"

A CONSTANT READER of Chinese Communist newspapers quickly learns one basic reason for the Peking regime's special hatred of the United States. Repeatedly those newspapers demand the "liberation of Taiwan from American imperialism." Repeatedly they ridicule the fact that China is represented in the United Nations by what the Chinese Communists call "the Chiang Kai-shek clique." They refer, of course, to the Government of Nationalist China, headed by President Chiang Kai-shek, with headquarters on the island of Taiwan. It is recognized as the legitimate Government of China by the United States and many other countries as well as by the United Nations.

To some it may seem strange that the rulers of

vast Mainland China, with its huge population, should be so concerned about Taiwan and the smaller islands under Chiang Kai-shek's rule. Taken together, all of these have an area not quite twice that of a small state such as New Jersey or New Hampshire, and their total population is about 12 million, less than that of New York State. It would seem that Mao Tse-tung could afford to ignore Taiwan rather than view it as a major irritant and problem, as he obviously does.

To understand Mao's concern about Taiwan, which is better known to many Americans as Formosa, let us try to put ourselves in his shoes by imagining how we would react if the positions were reversed. Suppose that Cuba, which is roughly as far from Florida as Taiwan is from the Southern China coast, were ruled not by Fidel Castro but by American Communists who claimed to constitute the legitimate Government of the United States. Suppose, too, that a Chinese Communist fleet patrolled the waters between Cuba and the United States with the intention of crushing any attack on Cuba launched by the United States. Suppose, finally, that the Government of Cuba boasted periodically that it was preparing to invade the United States and conquer it. Under these circumstances would not the Government and people of the United States be even more concerned about Cuba than they have been in recent years? Let us remember that even without the imaginary Chinese fleet on patrol off the Florida coast, Washington became so alarmed about Soviet missiles in Cuba in late 1962 that President Kennedy put the world on the brink of thermonuclear war to force the Russians to remove them.

Mao's concern about Taiwan can be explained in still another way. The existence of an independent Chinese Government there threatens Peking because it offers the Mainland Chinese possible alternatives—an alternative government, an alternative economic system, an alternative way of life. Mao can never feel completely secure as long as a rival regime claims to speak for China. Moreover, since the first days of the Korean War, Taiwan has been protected by the United States Seventh Fleet, which patrols the Formosa Strait. The Chiang Kai-shek regime is therefore a persistent reminder to Peking of its inability to defy the United States. In addition, there is for Mao the constant possibility that the United States and Chiang Kai-shek together may attack Mainland China, using Taiwan as their base. For all these reasons Mao worries about tiny Taiwan.

There is a good deal of evidence to suggest that the United States Government would like to change this situation. Many in Washington understand that it may not be possible for the United States to guard Taiwan indefinitely. Now that the Chinese Communists have demonstrated their ability to construct atomic weapons, it cannot be many years before Peking has the nuclear strength to destroy the Seventh Fleet and every living thing on Taiwan. Presumably the Chinese Communists would hesitate to do this for fear of American retaliation, but the very possibility that this may happen will strengthen their hand in the future. It would seem wise to work out an honorable settlement before Peking has a nuclear bargaining lever.

One proposal has received much attention. This is the "Two Chinas" plan by which the Governments of both Communist China and Taiwan would be generally recognized and permitted to belong to the United Nations, with the Peking regime taking over China's seat in the Security Council. It would require the two Governments to recognize each other and pledge to maintain peaceful relations. In the abstract this plan has virtues. It would probably appeal to many people on Taiwan who would like to be citizens of an independent country and who feel little or no loyalty to Mainland China. But so far it has run into an insuperable obstacle: It is rejected equally by both the Chinese Communist rulers and the Chiang Kai-shek regime. For all their differences, both groups insist that Taiwan is and must always remain a part of China —and each, of course, claims to be the only legitimate Government of all China, the mainland and

Taiwan together.

Officially the Chiang regime claims to be preparing to reconquer the mainland by force. A disproportionately large army is maintained in constant training for this purpose. From time to time groups of saboteurs and spies are dispatched to harass the Chinese Communists. Nationalist planes fly over the mainland to drop propaganda leaflets and to obtain intelligence information through aerial photography. Two islands controlled by Taiwan, Quemoy and Matsu, are very close to the southern China coast and from time to time engage in artillery duels with the mainland. Occasionally there have been reports that Chiang Kai-shek sought to mount invasions of Communist China, but if so he has been prevented by the United States, which supplies most of his troops' armament and pays much of the cost of maintaining them. In effect the United States tries to maintain a cease-fire in the area, keeping both sides from attacking each other.

Basic to the policy of the Chiang Government since it fled to Taiwan at the end of 1949 has been an effort to build up the island as a showcase for comparison with Communist China. The hope has been that a prosperous and stable society on Taiwan will demonstrate to the people of Communist China that the Nationalist regime is preferable to Mao Tse-tung's.

A good deal of progress has been achieved. Thus

a Government-sponsored land-reform program has made most of the farmers on Taiwan owners of their own farms. Investment in new industries has been vigorously pressed. So have medical care, education and steps designed to make Taiwan's agriculture more scientific and productive. In carrying out these and related measures the Nationalist Government has had help from the United States, which has provided large sums of money to finance many of the improvements.

The results have been impressive. The standard of living on Taiwan is now one of the highest in Asia. Industrial growth is easing the island's earlier dependence on the production and export of sugar cane and rice. The death rate has fallen sharply, giving the island one of the world's highest rates of population increase. A small group of Taiwanese millionaires and a new middle class have begun to emerge. Many an observer visiting the island and noting its progress cannot help but wonder what would have happened in China if, decades ago, on the mainland, Chiang Kai-shek had shown such imagination and willingness to institute reforms. But all that is water over the dam.

Politically Taiwan is a one-party dictatorship, the one party being the Kuomintang, which is dominated by Chiang. The Government's secret police sedulously hunt both Communist spies and Taiwanese trying to organize groups to advance purely

Taiwanese interests. The Chinese from the mainland who came to Taiwan with Chiang are an aging
group, but they occupy the key positions in the
Government.

There are understandable tensions between the
former mainlanders and the native Taiwanese.
Many of the latter still remember with resentment
the looting of their island which took place right
after World War II, when the Japanese left and the
men Chiang Kai-shek sent in proved to be carpet-
baggers interested only in enriching themselves.
Many of the Chinese, on the other hand, think
wistfully of returning to the mainland to die in
the home of their ancestors. Chinese Communist
broadcasts are aimed at these people, seeking to
foster defeatism among them and promising them
complete forgiveness if they desert Chiang and return home. Occasionally this appeal works and one
of Chiang's pilots or one of his representatives
abroad defects to Peking. Sometimes, however, the
defection is in the other direction and a Communist
Chinese pilot lands his plane on Taiwan or a Communist Chinese diplomat deserts his post abroad
and seeks asylum with the Nationalists.

Only the future will tell whether Taiwan can be
kept free of Communist China. Meanwhile, its people enjoy a life that is richer and less regimented
than the existence of the Mainland Chinese. In return for the protection and aid it provides, the

United States has in Taiwan a military and intelligence base that is a keystone of the entire American position in the western Pacific. It seems inconceivable that any Government of the United States would voluntarily turn the Taiwanese over to Peking's rule against their will. But what should be done if the Chinese Communists organize a successful revolution on the island, or if they threaten to use nuclear weapons against the Seventh Fleet? This question seems academic now, but it may not be in the future if the impasse over Taiwan, the "Second China," remains unresolved for too many more years.

X

The Future of Communist China

A FAVORITE SCIENCE-FICTION THEME is what man's first flight to the planets of another star—say, Alpha Centauri—will be like a century or more from now. Usually the crew of the space ship is envisioned as representing all of humanity—an African pilot, perhaps, and an American co-pilot, a Chinese navigator, a Brazilian communications man and so forth. The assumption, of course, is that mankind will have found a way to cooperate and that China in particular will have emerged as a peaceful member of the world community working with other countries on space exploration and similar matters of common interest.

There is another, very different vision of the future China. Napoleon Bonaparte warned the West

150 years ago against meddling with that country. China, he argued, was a sleeping dragon that had best be left to slumber lest it destroy those who awaken it. The empire-seekers who came after Napoleon disregarded his advice and today we must deal with the aroused dragon. Was Napoleon right in his forebodings, or is truth on the side of the science-fiction writers who foresee an era of glorious cooperation?

It is still too early to tell. For the moment, however, one thing is clear: Today's masters of Mainland China call themselves Communists, but their words and actions reveal them to be in effect the latest in the long line of emperors and imperial officials who ruled the land for many centuries. They have fused the evangelical zeal of Communism with Chinese national pride and arrogance. They dream of making China once again "The Middle Kingdom," the center of the world, from which supreme power will be exercised over the "barbarians" near and far. Their ambition is sharpened by a determination to avenge the humiliation and exploitation their nation suffered during the past century and more at the hands of both Westerners and Russians. China has, of course, made it plain that it does not accept the Russian seizure of more than 500,000 square miles of Chinese territory in the 19th century and demands its return. But even more disturbing to Moscow must be the hints from

Peking that it regards Russians as Europeans who have no just place beyond the Urals and must sooner or later retire behind them and surrender the vast area that is now Soviet Asia.

On the world scene China today appears as a major force seeking to extend its influence in every continent. Long the victim of imperialism, it now looms as a hungry imperialist scheming to gain territory and influence. Already it has won a satellite in Europe (Albania) and two in Asia (North Vietnam and North Korea). Two non-Communist lands, Cambodia and Indonesia, have linked their destinies with China's, apparently convinced that the United States will be driven from Asia, leaving the Chinese completely dominant there. In Burma, Thailand, the Philippines and elsewhere along the vast rim of China more and more statesmen and ambitious politicians are wondering whether it is not time to jump aboard Peking's bandwagon. Their attitude is traceable to the humiliating setbacks the United States has suffered in South Vietnam at the hands of the Chinese-supported Vietcong rebels and to Communist China's emergence as the first nonwhite nuclear power.

Today China offers itself in Asia, Africa and Latin America as the would-be leader of the "have not" nations against the "haves." It woos poor and underdeveloped countries with propaganda, economic assistance and arms. Simultaneously it trains revolutionaries. The influence of Chinese-trained Africans is already apparent, notably in Tanzania and the troubled Congo. In Latin America, too, there is an affinity between the Chinese and the extreme radicals who aspire to overthrow conservative or middle-of-the-road governments. In Venezuela, Colombia, Peru and other South American countries pro-Peking groups dream of winning power the way Mao Tse-tung did—through a revolution carried out by armies formed from peasants.

Perhaps the most ominous element in China's current strategy is the deliberate use of racism as a major political weapon. For the old Marxist slogan "Workers of the World Unite," Peking substitutes in effect "Colored People of the World Unite." And the Chinese offer themselves as the leaders of all nonwhites. More or less subtly the Chinese argue that for 500 years the white nations of the world have robbed, exploited and humiliated the nonwhites and the time has come to gain revenge. Both the United States and the Soviet Union are targets. Discrimination and violence against Negroes in the United States is exploited by Chinese propaganda throughout Asia, Africa and Latin America to "prove" that the United States really stands for the domination of whites over nonwhites. Similarly, Peking argues that the nonwhite peoples of the Soviet Union are the subjects and puppets of the whites, the Russians. At leftist international conferences in

Asia and Africa the Chinese have more than once told the Russians they had no place in the assemblages because they were whites. In the public debates between China and the Soviet Union during 1963–1964 the Russians frequently made plain their alarm over the racist nature of Peking's tactics. They protested that the Chinese were trying to replace the Marxist doctrine of class struggle based on economic divisions—workers vs. employers—with the idea of struggle based on divisions of color and geography.

Chinese racism is, of course, a highly cynical device. Peking welcomes the support of white people where it is available, as among the pro-Chinese white Communists in Albania, New Zealand and other countries. Moreover, Mao and his cohorts have shown no hesitation in using violence against nonwhites when it suited their purpose. The brutal repression of the people of Tibet and Sinkiang when they sought independence from China in the nineteen-fifties and early nineteen-sixties is one example. Another is the Chinese attack on India in 1962. African students who have studied at Chinese universities report that many ordinary Chinese are as race-conscious and race-proud as the most bigoted white men in the southern United States or South Africa. Nevertheless, in many areas Chinese racist propaganda is effective because many people still recall with resentment the arrogance and injustice of their former white colonial masters. But those who are swayed by Chinese racism do not stop to think that the ultimate purpose of Peking's propaganda is to substitute Chinese masters for the departed white rulers.

How realistic are Communist China's dreams of world power and world empire?

In the short run, during the years immediately ahead, they are certainly unrealistic. Militarily China is still very weak compared with the United States and the Soviet Union. Both the latter countries are major nuclear powers capable of effectively destroying China if the need ever arose. The United States and the Soviet Union have literally thousands and tens of thousands of the most powerful nuclear weapons and the planes and long-range missiles to deliver them. The Chinese have at most a few atomic bombs and virtually no long-range planes and missiles. Peking's chief military asset is still conventional infantry. It can throw huge hordes of soldiers into battle, but they can be used only against China's immediate neighbors on the Asian mainland. Peking does not have the ships or air-power to move large forces even across the short stretch of sea separating China from Japan, let alone across the immense Pacific. China can exert military pressure against the Soviet Union, India and Southeast Asia, but in the near future it cannot be a major military factor in Africa, Europe or the

Western Hemisphere.

Furthermore, China's economic weakness will continue for many years to impose strict restraints on its leaders' ambitions. In the mid-nineteen-sixties China's economy is significantly stronger than it was in the bad days of 1960–1962, when mass starvation threatened, but this still represents grinding poverty. The Chinese people, like people everywhere, want more of the material things of life, and this pressure cannot be wholly ignored by their rulers. Moreover, if China is ever to be a major power it must tremendously expand its pitifully small industrial complex. China, with more than 700 million people, now has a volume of industrial production comparable perhaps to that of such smaller countries of Europe as Belgium or the Netherlands—and even this comparison may exaggerate Chinese industrial strength. It will take many years of great effort before China can be an industrial nation rivaling the United States, the Soviet Union, Japan, Britain, France or West Germany.

In the longer run, however, the possibility of China's becoming a global power capable of exerting enormous pressure in many parts of the world cannot be dismissed. The key factor here is whether Peking can develop large stockpiles of atomic and hydrogen bombs and the planes, missiles and submarines to deliver them anywhere. If a weak China has been able to cause so much trouble in Asia and Africa in recent years, we may take it for granted that a much stronger China in the nineteen-seventies and nineteen-eighties represents a threat indeed. There are already observers who predict that World War III will be fought between China on one side and the United States and the Soviet Union on the other.

What should be done about the problem Communist China poses for the rest of the world? There are many points of view, of course, but two main ones illustrate the range of alternatives before the United States and other nations.

One school of thought regards the present Chinese aggressiveness and hate propaganda as an expression of the anger which more than a century of foreign injustices has produced. Those who hold this point of view argue that the way to transform China into a responsible and constructive member of the world community is to redress justified grievances and offer Peking concrete advantages if it shows itself willing to cooperate in creating and maintaining international stability. Thus it is suggested that Communist China be admitted to the United Nations and be given Nationalist China's seat on the Security Council. Some people suggest that Taiwan itself be handed over to Peking. Finally, it is suggested that the richer countries combine to offer Communist China large amounts of economic aid so it can speed industrialization and raise its people's standard of living more rapidly.

Those who oppose these ideas contend that there are no visible limits to the Chinese appetite. They deny that Peking would be satisfied merely with the return of Taiwan and a seat on the United Nations Security Council. They point to Chinese claims on Mongolia, on much of Soviet Asia, on Southeast Asia, on large areas along the border with India. Won't China's appetite simply grow with every concession? they ask. Moreover, they say, what right has anyone to give Taiwan to Communist China against the wishes of the Taiwanese people? And would it not be suicidal, they add, to help China industrialize and thus increase its ability to become a truly modern military power quickly?

At the opposite extreme from advocacy of aid to Peking is a policy line pushed by those who believe that a militarily and economically strong China would be catastrophic for the rest of the world. This school of thought stresses the dangers posed by the prospect that China will have a billion or more people soon. It argues that when China has the power it will demand a major redistribution of the world's land and other resources to give the Chinese their "fair share." In this view, the Chinese, who will make up almost a third of the world's population, will never be satisfied in the long run unless they have at least the same fraction of the world's territory, wealth and power. And this, it is argued, can be obtained only by taking territory, wealth and power away from those who have what the Chinese consider "more than their fair share." On a population basis, of course, the United States, the Soviet Union and the countries of both Western and Eastern Europe all have more than a proportionate share of the world's resources.

The solution, these hard-liners assert, lies in keeping China weak. They argue, for example, that the United States and the Soviet Union, alone or together, should act to destroy all Chinese nuclear weapons factories and other key military production plants. It will be disastrous for both the American and the Soviet peoples, they contend, if China is allowed to become a major nuclear power. That, they say, must be prevented at all costs.

Those who oppose such a policy argue that it is immoral to think of waging a preventive war against China. Moreover, they hold, any such war would be futile, since it is fantastic to suppose that for all future time the vast mass of Chinese humanity can be denied the weapons and technology other nations possess. Finally, the skeptics assert that the Soviet Union and the United States are simply too suspicious and fearful of each other to work together, even in their common interest against China.

There were echoes of this debate in the major speech President Johnson delivered on April 7,

1965, when he defined American policy and goals in Vietnam. On the one hand, the President pointed to Communist China as the real enemy inspiring the Vietcong rebels in South Vietnam and their North Vietnamese suppliers and allies. The President said:

Over this war and all Asia is another reality: the deepening shadow of Communist China. The rulers in Hanoi are urged on by Peking. This is a regime which has destroyed freedom in Tibet, which has attacked India and which has been condemned by the United Nations for aggression in Korea.

It is a nation which is helping the forces of violence in almost every continent. The contest in Vietnam is part of a wider pattern of aggressive purposes.

The hard-liners could argue that the President's words really imply taking as tough a posture toward China as necessary before she develops her own nuclear arsenal.

But in the same speech the President called for peace in Vietnam and proposed a billion-dollar investment in all the countries of Southeast Asia, including North Vietnam. Those who oppose the hard-liners could argue that this Johnson Plan—so reminiscent of the Marshall Plan, by which the United States helped Western European economic recovery in the late nineteen-forties—is the way toward lasting peace. If peace in Southeast Asia is worth a billion dollars to the United States, would not peace with China be worth an investment of several billion dollars in Chinese economic development?

The President's speech won much applause, but there were discordant voices. Some Americans deplored his idea, calling it an attempt at bribery and a reward for aggression. North Vietnam, Communist China and the Soviet Union all denounced it.

Yet an idea of great potential had been born. The President of the United States had planted a seed that will be hard to kill, though it may take time before it sprouts and sends green shoots above the earth. Certainly he must have touched many hearts in every land when he said:

For most of history, men have hated and killed one another in battle. But we dream of an end to war. We will try to make it so.

For all existence, most men have lived in poverty, threatened by hunger. But we dream of a world where all are fed and charged with hope. And we will help to make it so.

The ordinary men and women of North Vietnam and South Vietnam, of China and India, of Russia and America, are brave people. They are filled with the same proportions of hate and fear, of love and hope. Most of them want the same things for themselves and their families. Most of them do not want their sons to ever die in battle, or to see their homes or the homes of others destroyed.

Well, this can be their world yet. Man now has the knowledge—always before denied—to make this planet serve the real needs of the people who live on it.

It seems fitting to conclude by considering the current Chinese leaders' expectations about the future. These were made explicit not long ago. The future, the Chinese Communists announced, will be one of long-drawn-out struggle, sacrifice and effort. The drive to build full Communism in China and to win the entire world for Communism will take a tremendous amount of time. As the Chinese Communists wrote in 1964:

> Success requires anywhere from one to several centuries. On the question of duration, it is better to prepare for a longer rather than a shorter period of time. On the question of effort, it is better to regard the task as difficult rather than easy.

The emphasis now in Communist China is on training the younger generation to be faithful to Communism and to carry on the work begun by

Mao Tse-tung—in his manner and toward his goals. It is clear that Mao and his colleagues—most of them in their sixties and seventies—were deeply alarmed late in 1963 when an American official suggested that after the present rulers died a new generation of more moderate Chinese leaders would appear, a generation willing to make peace with the United States and live as good neighbors with the rest of the world. To Mao this seemed a prediction that Communism in China would "degenerate," as he believes Communism in the Soviet Union has "degenerated" since Stalin's death. He is making every effort to assure that those who come after him will continue, not abandon, his policies.

But Mao has his doubts about whether the China of the future will follow his road after he has gone. Speaking to the American writer Edgar Snow in early 1965, Mao said that the life of man on earth was changing with increasing rapidity. He speculated that a thousand years from now all the leaders of the past century, even Marx, Engels and Lenin, might seem rather ridiculous. What he was implying, of course, was that at some time in the future the Chinese may even think that Mao was ridiculous. Put another way, Mao fears he may be repudiated by his own people after his death as Stalin was repudiated in the Soviet Union after he died in 1953.

There is ground for Mao's fear. His dreams of global revolution, his bitterness against the outside world, his willingness to sacrifice present comfort for future power are the products of his own experience and China's history during the 20th century. But such concerns are far from the mind of the average Chinese, who is oppressed every day by the poverty of his existence and who dreams, like poor men everywhere, of a better life for himself and his children. When Mao dies there will be no one of comparable prestige to replace him. There may be rivalry and competition among those who would succeed him. In that new situation the desires of the Chinese people will have far greater influence than they have now. And those desires are much more likely to be gratified in an era of peace and international cooperation than in an era of hostility and a continuing arms race.

Even more fundamentally, the hydrogen bomb poses for the Chinese, as it does for all of us, these two alternatives: coexistence or coextinction. The Chinese people no more want to be wiped out in a nuclear war than do the people of any other country. Sooner or later there must be a government in Peking that will come to terms with the realities of the nuclear age. When that time comes the way will be open for the great Chinese people to rejoin the rest of mankind in a great, cooperative march forward for the benefit of all humanity. The way ahead, no doubt, will be long, tortuous and dangerous. But this writer, for one, is willing to bet that there will be a Chinese aboard when the first manned spaceship sets off for Alpha Centauri.

INDEX

HARRY SCHWARTZ

Harry Schwartz was born in New York City. He attended Columbia University on a Pulitzer Scholarship, was valedictorian of the Class of 1940, Junior Phi Beta Kappa and won the Mitchell Fellowship. He received his M.A. and Ph.D. from Columbia University too. He has served with the United States Department of State, the Office of Strategic Services and the Department of Agriculture. He was professor of economics in the Maxwell School of Syracuse University and has taught also at Columbia, New York University, American University and Brooklyn College. He has lectured on problems related to Communism at the National War College, Harvard, Yale, Princeton, Cornell, Johns Hopkins and other major universities. He began writing on Communism for *The New York Times* in 1947 and has been a member of the *Times* Editorial Board and its expert on Communist affairs since 1951. He has traveled extensively through the Communist world.

DATE DUE

DISPLAY			
JAN 11 '83			
FEB 1 5 1983			
GAYLORD			PRINTED IN U.S.A.